What People are Saying about…

A Desperate God

"This is a game changer. In just the first chapter, Clay gives us an overview of the first 4000 years of human history. He presents God as a true lover of humanity, a Father (desperately) longing, sometimes even sadly, for the love of his children. This is a fresh and resoundingly uplifting way of viewing a God. And, for me, a final piece of the puzzle that fits perfectly!'– **Joe Moore,** *author, screenwriter and entrepreneur, founder of Moore Innovations.*

Clay is a man of faith and when he prays he prays in faith and believes. He encourages us to pray as Jesus directed that He will do whatever we ask in His name, so that the Father may be glorified in the Son. We may ask Him for anything in His name, and He will do it. -- **Mike Kolen,** *former linebacker at Auburn and member of Miami Dolphins only undefeated team in NFL history.*

Just one thing to say…This book is engaging and well written. Even though I don't personally know the people in the book, I felt close to them through the telling of their journey. The journey with God will inevitably include times when our trust that He hears our prayers is seriously challenged. We have found that it's then that hearing other's personal accounts of how God answered their prayers is one thing that can build our faith and help us keep pressing on in prayer. You will find that kind of help in A Desperate God. – **Steve Chapman,** *author, member of the Christian folk band Dogwood and Steve and Annie Chapman.*

God is always faithful. Even in our darkest hour and lowest moments. He is faithful. I love the book and how it increases my faith to hear stories of how God has been faithful to answer prayers in another person's life. Of course, it is always encouraging to read the chapter in this book how He answered a prayer for me. —**Chandler Mosely,** *Student Chaplin for Faulkner University.*

A Desperate God

Discovering Father God Through the Answered Prayers of a Nobody

Clay J. Mize

A Desperate God

Published by Thorn Hill Books

117 Lakewood Drive

Sheffield, AL 35660

All rights reserved. No part of this publication may be reproduced, stored in a retrieval system, or transmitted in any form or by any means—for example, electronic, photocopy, recording—without the prior written permission of the author. The only exception is for brief quotations in printed reviews.

All Scripture quotations, unless otherwise indicated, are taken from the New King James Version®, Copyright ©1982, 2010, by Thomas Nelson, Inc. Used by permission. All rights reserved.

ISBN-13:978-0692148501

ISBN-10:0692148507

© 2018 by Clay Mize

THORN HILL
BOOKS

Acknowledgements

I would like to express my appreciation to my friends and mentors who joined my advisor team to help me through the editing process. Though the advisor team helped in many ways the views in this book are my own and do not necessarily reflect the beliefs of those on the team. To the contrary, several team members voiced concerns to several of my views and ideas and a few requested their names be left out. Those brave souls who joined with me and did not object to being included are in alphabetic order are:

Roger Burdge, Drew Brooks, Mark Bates, Dan Burgess, Jamey Congleton, Bill Biggs, Janie Darby, Sloan Dickerson, Tim Evans, Steve Humphries, Johnny Frazier, Heidi King, Pete Key, Kevin Knight, Bart Kirshler, Soni Likens, Deana Linderholm, Anita Lyons, Daniel Lyles, Boo Mason, Mark Maybrey, Joey Mustain, Larry Marshall, Sandy McMurtrey, Jeanette Masdon, Joe Moore, Lamar Miller, Shevelia McGuire, Chandler Moseley, James McCarley, Andrew McCarley, Marshall Neal, Cathy Smith Nelson, Rebecca Postell, Jim Richards, Chris Stokes, Rex Snyder, Susan Thomason, John Tsironis, and Dana Wallace.

I owe a debt of gratitude to my Sunday night fellowship group who were my guinea pigs as I shared these ideas and stories of answered prayers. They helped me remember the answers and refine the story telling. There are others who helped, but due to their humility requested to remain nameless.

Table of Contents

Section I – Laying the Foundation 13

1: Why Do We Need to Pray? 15

2: Why God Didn't Answer Your Prayer 31

3: What Are You Praying For? 41

4: What Prayers Has God Answered For You? 47

5: Why You Don't Have What You Want 51

Section II: Answered Prayers of a Nobody 57

6: Now I Lay Me Down to Sleep 59

7: When You Want to Quit 65

8: Forgiveness is Given but Trust is Earned 77

9: The Unexpected Consequence of an Answered Prayer 91

10: Three Winks 103

11: Self-Substantiation What in the World Is That? 109

12: Sometimes We Are Not Ready for the Answer 117

13: There is No Victory Without a Battle 127

14: Mama Prayed 135

15: Learning to Follow the Nudge of the Spirit 143

16: The Hem of Your Garment 155

17: My Guardian Angel 163

18: A Painful Learning Curve 169

19: I Don't Want This Business Anymore, You Can Have It 177

20: The Wayward Wife 185

21: Father, Tell Me How Much You Love Me 193

22: My Dad's Last Day 201

23: Tell Cher I Love Her 209

24: A Billion Dollar View 217

25: God Must Really Like This Cat 223

26: A Gift for Healing 229

27: Laying On Hands 237

28: The Man You Intended 245

29: Prayers of the Ego 253

About the Author 257

I have this recurring dream. I am standing alone before the great judge of the world at the end of days. He asks me, "What do you have to offer me from your life on earth? Why should I allow you into this land called Heaven?"

I look at Him and say, "I have no body of work that survived the fire. My hands are empty."

Yet, I think to myself, there is something...

Section I – Laying the Foundation

1

Why Do We Need to Pray?

"WHY DO WE NEED TO PRAY?" Jerry asked at our coffee group one morning. "I mean, really. That may sound like a dumb question, but I'm serious. If God is in control, if He lives outside of time and sees the end from the beginning, if He doesn't change and His mind can't be changed, then why do we need to pray? It seems pointless."

H.L, our eldest member at age 85, suffers with Parkinson's and has a very soft voice. When he spoke, we all leaned in. He chuckled and said, "You just do because the Bible tells us to." For about 50% of the group, that answer was sufficient. For the rest of us, we continued to hammer out the details every day at coffee for weeks to come.

Back to the Beginning

The essence of why we need to pray took us all the way back to the beginning. We needed to learn what the mind and intent of God was in creating man. What we learned was that God created mankind in His own likeness or image. Another way of saying this is that God has a son and calls him Adam.[1]

---

[1] Luke 3:38

Soon after, God gives Adam a wife, created for him, and out of him.[2] He also gave Adam and Eve responsibility.[3] In keeping with their status as children of God, God made them to rule. They were to rule over the entire plant and animal kingdom and every creature. They were also charged to have children to fill up the earth and bring it under their control.[4]

This was the will of God. He gave the earth to mankind, to care for it and bring it under His control. In the beginning, God delegated. King David said it like this:

> *You made them a little lower than the angels; you crowned them with glory and honor and put everything under their feet. In putting everything under them, God left nothing that is not subject to them (Psalms 8:5-6).*

Soon we learn that God is not a micromanager. He will allow Adam and Eve to rule as they see fit, even to the point of allowing them to make a fatal mistake.[5]

The next scene in our journey of discovery takes us to the Garden of Eden. The Garden is a place planted by God for Adam and Eve to live. It was a beautiful place for them to tend and begin their undertaking.

Eventually, a serpent who is craftier than all other wild animals shows up to tempt Eve.[6] We all know what comes next. The serpent tempts Eve to take the forbidden fruit from the Tree of the Knowledge of Good and Evil, and thus becomes more like God, knowing both good and evil. However, with Adam and Eve's disobedience comes consequences -- one being the curse of the ground. Man's food source

---

[2] Genesis 2:22
[3] Genesis 2:15
[4] Genesis 1:28
[5] Genesis 3:6
[6] Genesis 3:1

is cursed, and because of it, man will die and return to the ground. The Bible says it like this:

> *You will eat food by the sweat of your brow until you're buried in the ground, because you were taken from it. You're made from dust and you'll return to dust (Genesis 3:19).*

The Effects of the Fall

Through the curse, mankind is introduced to struggle. The effects of this struggle are devastating, as man attempts to control his environment in his own way. Carried away with the knowledge of evil and its pleasures, man begins to forget God. More than ever, man needs God's help and guidance, but instead of more help, sin has all but destroyed man's previous level of relationship and communication with God. Lucky for us, there is nothing worse for our Heavenly Father than for His children to forget who He is.

There is a lot our coffee group didn't understand about the role Satan plays on the earth, but we learned his role has been significant since the Garden of Eden and will continue to be until he is cast out after the final judgment.

Here are a few things we learned:

Mankind is born into a dominion of darkness.

> *He has delivered us from the dominion of darkness and transferred us to the kingdom of His beloved Son (Colossians 1:13).*

Since the time of Adam, man has become a slave to sin.

> *Jesus answered them, "Truly, truly, I say to you, everyone who commits sin is a slave to sin" (John 8:34).*

Apostle Paul calls Satan the god of this world.

> *In their case, the god of this world has blinded the minds of the unbelievers, to keep them from seeing the light of the gospel*

of the glory of Christ, who is the image of God (II Corinthians 4:4).

Satan oppresses people.

How God anointed Jesus of Nazareth with the Holy Spirit and with power; how He went about doing good and healing all that were oppressed by the devil, for God was with Him (Acts 10:38).

Impure and evil spirits live in people.

When an impure spirit comes out of a person, it goes through arid places seeking rest and does not find it (Matthew 12:43).

We also learn Satan has access to both man and God, for he constantly accuses the believer of wrongdoing before God.

And I heard a loud voice saying in heaven, "Now is come salvation, and strength, and the kingdom of our God, and the power of His Christ, for the accuser of our brethren is cast down, which accused them before our God day and night" (Revelation 12:10).

We concluded mankind is in deep trouble. We are born into a dominion of darkness where Satan is god. He remains a major influencer of mankind. He oppresses people; evil spirits live in people who are already slaves to sin. Satan has plenty of legitimate reasons to go before God regarding His creation and accuse mankind of wrongdoing.

So Where Is God in All This Chaos, We Asked?

The more we searched for answers, the more we saw the scriptures as God's letters (revelation) to man about what He is doing to rescue us from our perilous situation. It has become increasingly clear that God is depending on man to reclaim the earth for God. It is God's will and plan for man to help redeem what has been lost or spoiled.

We took a fly-over view from 30,000 feet and plotted a summary of how God has used man to redeem His creation and save mankind.

After the curse, the first generations of man on earth became progressively evil. Every inclination of the thoughts of their heart were evil continually.[7] Earth was corrupt and full of violence.[8] In a desperate move, God repented that He ever made man and decided it was time to start over.[9]

However, confirming his great love for man, God chose a man, Noah, to begin again. In time, he would choose another man, Abraham, who distinguished himself by his faith in God. God would promise Abraham that all the nations of the earth would be blessed through one of his descendants.[10] Some 400 years later, God chose Moses to give and administer the law to help shape a nation from Abraham's descendants.[11] God continued to choose people we call the prophets to communicate His plans. Then at the center of human history, God chose for Jesus, His Son, to become a man and come to earth, to demonstrate the splendor of His love and accomplish the solution to save mankind.

One of the many things we learned about God's will is that He sent Jesus into the world not to condemn the world but to save it.[12] Jesus proclaimed that God has anointed Him to proclaim the good news to the poor, freedom for the prisoner, recovery of sight to the blind, to set the oppressed free, and finally proclaim the year of the Lord's favor.[13]

---

[7] Genesis 6:5
[8] Genesis 6:11
[9] Genesis 6:5-8
[10] Genesis 18:18
[11] Exodus 11:1-17
[12] John 3:17
[13] Luke 4:18-19

Jesus said He only did on earth what He first saw the Father doing.[14] So, we learned that God the Father's will for earth is only good, for Jesus went about doing only good. Apostle John goes on to tell us the reason the Son of God appeared was to destroy the devil's work.[15] For us to understand the intentions of God toward man and the will of God in action, we now have two great examples. The first is man's time in the Garden before sin and the curse, and the second is to observe the actions of Jesus while on earth.

It was a relief to learn that all the bad that happens on earth is not God's will, but the result of sin, the curse upon the earth, and the works of the devil. Now God chooses men and women (believers) to spread His solution, one man and one woman at a time, and make disciples out of them.[16]

Obviously, the task is immense and is one of the reasons it is so important for us to pray. God counts on people, ready to take their place of authority and dominion, to do and ask for God's will to be done upon the earth.[17] This, of course, requires a man who has come to realize who he is.

To understand who we are and the charge of our mission, we must be delivered from this darkened conditioned and be transformed.[18][19] This transformation includes being equipped with the life of Jesus through the Holy Spirit,[20][21] being ransomed from the bondage of sin,[22] redeemed from the curse of the law,[23] forgiven by God, and reconciled

---

[14] John 5:19
[15] I John 3:8
[16] Matthew 28:19
[17] Matthew 6:10
[18] Colossians 1:3
[19] II Corinthians 3:18
[20] Galatians 2:20
[21] John 6:63
[22] Matthew 20:28
[23] Galatians 3:13

to Him.[24][25] This new man trusts God and His will and calls it down to earth through prayer.

This explains the mystery in the model prayer where Jesus instructs us to ask for the Father's will to be done on earth as it is in heaven. What is the Father's will? As stated earlier, the first glimpse is life in the Garden prior to sin spoiling it, and the second is displayed in the life of Jesus. Much of what we witness today is far from the Father's will.

What remains a mystery is why the Lord waits to restore the Father's will on earth. Through His accomplishments as a man on earth, Jesus became our champion and was given all authority in heaven and on earth.[26] However, we know His plan is not complete. He waits.

One reason we know He waits is because He is not yet satisfied with the size of His family.[27] Also a mystery is why He allows Satan and his minions to remain on earth to influence people for evil. Why does He require for those He is to save to enter through the narrow gate of faith in Christ?

One explanation for why He waits, in addition to wanting more children, is by wisdom, He understands man's need to experience evil. Because of choice, did man need to be convinced that evil is bad? Apparently, Adam and Eve needed to learn this lesson. We also know that from Adam until the time He closes the door on new additions, that all men will experience evil and its consequences.

As the Lord waits, He leaves man to wrestle with evil powers for dominion over the earth for the time being. He sent His Spirit to indwell us who believe, but He also left the devil to provide an alternative -- evil. It is apparent that choice is a vital ingredient to the man God made.

---

[24] Ephesians 1:7
[25] II Corinthians 5:18
[26] Matthew 28:18
[27] Romans 11:25

So why is it important to ask for the Father's will to be done? It is our choice. Prior to His second coming, we still need to choose who we agree with and whose fellowship we desire. God's desire is for us to prefer His fellowship, His ways, and His will. Before His return, if man doesn't do or request the Father's will, the natural consequence of this fallen world and its evil systems prevail.

So, we concluded, we need God and God needs us. At God's design, we are partners for taking back the earth for God; He needs not only our actions to comply with His will, but our calling forth the will of God on earth. We are His boots on the ground in close combat, and our mission is to call down air support wherever we see a need for God's will, as we spread the word of His solution (salvation) and make disciples. We are *special forces behind enemy lines* working directly for the King. Though He has revealed what He plans to do and how the story ends, we do not know who or how many we may help navigate safely to the other shore.

How the Sovereignty of God Works

Maggie (not her real name) is a friend and on my advisor team. She had the following concern after reading this chapter. I should add that my views are not necessarily the views of my advisor team.

Maggie: I am a little confused when you say God's will is not being done. Nothing can thwart God's purposes. God's will is His will, with or without me. The apostle Paul's life was interrupted on his way to persecute Christians.

The sovereign God overrules the plans of man to fulfill His purposes. According to Proverbs 16:9, He doesn't need me to request His will in order to fulfill it. There are many examples in scripture where God intervened and worked His will without anyone's input. He works in people's hearts as He pleases. See the following verses: I Kings 12:15, Proverbs 21:1, Jeremiah 1:5, Jeremiah 10:23, Daniel 5:23-24.

Clay: Obviously, we are not the first people to discuss how the sovereignty of God works. There are multiple viewpoints. Hopefully, this will shed some light, or at least understanding, of the viewpoints. It is helpful to our understanding to realize that honest people have read the scriptures and formed very different views. It can be enlightening to first look at the two polar opposite views.

At one pole is the view associated with deist. God is a great clockmaker. He created the clock and does not interfere with His creation until the end of time that only He knows. In this view, this is God's sovereign will, to allow man's will to predominate until He returns.

At the other pole is a view associated with those called hyper-Calvinists. This is the belief that God is in control of everything. Nothing happens without God orchestrating it. He is orchestrating all events, both good and bad, like a great conductor. In this view, even the saved and lost have no choice.

Before moving to my view, I think it is important to add that this topic will not become crystal clear until the Lord returns.

I will call the view I ascribe to *the divine gentleman view*. God, as the divine gentleman, has given man dominion over the earth. Why? He doesn't tell us precisely but does give intimations.[28]

God, as a divine gentleman, desires to help but does not control the affairs of man. When the Lord made man, one of the chief distinguishing characteristics He designed into us was a free will to do as we choose. He did not want robots. He gave us instructions to follow but did not force us to obey. What we witness in the world today is largely a result of the will of men. However, God has planted His Kingdom on earth and is taking back His creation and restoring full

---

[28] https://wp.me/p43B0F-tx

fellowship with His children. This plan always requires a man's desire for God's will and for God's help.

God chose a few, whose hearts He trusted, to reveal His plan. These were not perfect men, but men who, when it came down to it, wanted the Lord's will and plan. These men and women used their God-given authority as man to prophesy or speak God's plans and warnings into existence.

All the examples you mentioned could be understood through this view, and, at the same time, explain why there is so much suffering and heartache in the world and why the need to pray is so great. Prayer is not just something we do without consequence, while God controls everything like a grand puppet master. Instead, prayer is crucial and can prove to be the difference between God's will and the natural course of things under the curse.

The example of God's interrupting Paul's life, as well as the life of evil King Pharaoh and others, could all be understood and explained as God answering the prayers of His children.

Of course, finally, God sent the ultimate man, with the perfect heart for God, in the man Jesus. While here, He taught us to pray for God's will and to do His will. He didn't leave the impression that God's will was being done with or without Him. To the contrary, if Jesus had not chosen to do God's will at the cross, mankind would still be lost, or at least God would have had to come up with another plan. Jesus' willingness, His choice, makes Him all the more wonderful.

In the same way, if the Lord had told us to pray for God's will to be done, but His will is done whether we pray or not, then His instruction for us to pray for God's will is meaningless. My contention is that the Lord did not give us meaningless instructions.

Giving God a Bad Name

The view that causes the most damage to the cause of Christ is the hyper-Calvinist view. This is the view that God is in control of every detail of life. I recently had a conversation with an old college friend who holds this view. I read his blog about how God is in control of everything.

We are friends and I felt comfortable challenging him with an extreme example. I said, "You are not saying that God is controlling the actions of the pedophile to molest the little girl as we speak, are you?" I knew a hyper-Calvinist doesn't want to be trapped with that question, and we dropped the subject. It is a fair question, and correct doctrine shouldn't lead you into a trap that impugns the character and nature of God.

A Challenge to the Idea That God Has Needs

Thomas (not his real name) and I attend a Torah study at the local Jewish synagogue. It is attended by more Christians than Jews. During a discussion of this topic, Thomas challenged the premise that God has needs.

Thomas: God does not need us. God is holy, eternal, almighty, and totally self-sufficient. He does not need any created being. He is God. He has no needs and does not need us in any way.

Clay: That makes God so sterile and impossible to relate to. I personally believe He not only has needs, but His needs are great.

Thomas: I think you are mistaking a want for a need.

Clay: Do you have children?

Thomas: Yes.

Clay: Did you want children?

Thomas: Yes.

Clay: Do you have a good relationship with your children?

Thomas: Yes, and my grandchildren are my pride and joy.

Clay: Do you need your children and grandchildren?

Thomas: Well, yes, I do now. *(Laughter breaks out around the table.)*

Clay: Of course, you do. And to try to understand a Being whose primary quality is love outside the context of relationship is pointless. The God of the Bible does not act like a God with no needs. It is just the opposite. If you look at the actions of God toward man, He is acting like a person who is desperate.

A Desperate God

Think again about a God who allows His only begotten Son to permanently take human form and subject Him to torture, humiliation, and the cruellest death possible. And all for the sake of restoring His relationship with us. Those are signs of vulnerable desperation. Like an army who burned their ships on arrival, He has committed to His creation. A creation He designed with a powerful free will that makes Him vulnerable to our opposition and rebellion. He must save man, for He has Himself become a man.

These desperate acts tell me we have underestimated our value. This is the value He placed on us while we were still lost and blundering about in our sin and selfishness. Is it possible He could express even more love to the child who comes to Him for love and life? I love the words from the poet Jonathan David Helser. He writes *I have seen I AM and I know that I am loved. I have seen I AM and now I know who I am.* Until we know I AM, we cannot know how much we are loved or even know who we are. Who is a child without the identity derived from the love of her parents? In the Father's love, we find our true identity. We are nothing detached from that love. That love *is* our identity. We are lost. Our identity is lost when we don't know the love of our Father.

Remember the tragic stories we have of God in the Old Testament. How it must have pained *the Lord of Love* to orchestrate the killing of grandchildren who had forgotten Him and hardened their hearts against Him and His plan for redemption. These are the actions of a desperate God. Not desperate in that He is without power, but desperate to make the decisions necessary to save His creation, and desperate to orchestrate tragic events, destroying some to save others. This is a God who gives definition to the word *love* to mean both vulnerable and un-controlling. What vulnerability He must feel as one who loves with the heart of a father.

Some churchmen have unintentionally painted a picture of God the Father to be an in-control, passionless genius playing a great game in which we are all pawns. That person is easy to hate as he sits in judgment, all smug, without a single need, threatening eternal torture to his powerless, pitiful created subjects, while demanding worship. This is not the Father I know or will portray. It is understandable why many have denied the faith and rejected this aloof and angry old god depicted by some theologians. To see God as sovereign, before we see Him as a desperately passionate and *in love* Father, is to get the wrong idea of who He is.

The god with no need would prefer the cold, damp cathedrals of Europe, instead of the God who says His dwelling place is in the hearts of men and women who love Him. That sounds like a God who needs. He is not a God who needs us to serve Him, but wants us to serve Him, because He knows that service is the language of love. He doesn't need us to worship Him, but He knows that worship is what a heart filled with love does.

The god with no needs is no different from the carved idols the ancients worshipped out of superstition...a god to appease to keep their needs met or to keep from getting smashed. No wonder the worship of so many is so dull. It is the wrong god. There is no emotion in the worship of appeasement. This is not the God of scripture. Instead, we have anthropomorphized our hard, cool, and emotionless hearts on God. We imagine a power-centered God and not a love-centered God. As this father, he is the stern Georg von Trapp in *The Sound of Music*, full of rules and strict discipline.

But our God and Father is full of emotions. We know He gets angry, hates,[29] repents,[30] relents,[31] is sad,[32] and gets frustrated. He rejoices and laughs,[33] has expectations and becomes disappointed, and even changes His mind. These are not the characteristics of an emotionless god who is going through the motions with an unalterable future. Our Father, being one with Jesus, is the Lamb that was slain.

The HE IS

When Jesus revealed that to see and know Him was to see and know the Father, the *I AM* could now be stated as the HE IS. The character attributes we see in Jesus are the character attributes that belong to the Father. Therefore, HE IS the one who would stoop to wash the disciples' feet. HE IS the one who suffers insults without anger. HE IS the one who would not condemn the woman caught in adultery. HE IS the one who turned over the tables in anger when He saw the privileged taking advantage of the common man.

When we see that God has a desperate love need, does that in some way diminish His greatness? No way! He is greater than before. When we realize that even God is in desperate need for love and is vulnerable to our darts, then we wouldn't be so quick to harden our hearts toward Him or as quick to throw away any of our relationships.

---

[29] Proverbs 6:6-9
[30] Genesis 6:6
[31] Jonah 3:10
[32] Ezekiel 18:23
[33] Proverbs 2:4

Not only do we not flourish without love, there is no surviving without love in the long run.

There is an equality factor that comes into being when two persons love each other. We are never more equal to God than when He decided to love us. Now all the boundaries that apply to one who loves now apply to God. Once we enter into His love, He is bound by His character to be patient and kind, humble, not easily angered, and to keep no record of wrongs. Dare I mention He is also bound to His own idea of mutual submission, and in so being, He puts us before Himself? And at some point, after doing so much for us, does He develop an attitude that He is owed? I don't think so! Even though we owe Him everything, He is not that way. Instead, His love will always, in every instance, protect us, trust us, expect the best of us, persevere with us; and His love keeps giving and never fails.

Most of us underestimate our love need. There is a reason we are born into families. There is a reason we are social creatures who seek friendships. There is a reason we fall in love, marry, and have children. There is a reason that our hearts are broken when these relationships fail. It is here that we bear God's image.

So, why do we need to pray? Because He asked us, and He needs us to. Why? Because, like any good Father, He is desperate for the well-being of His beloved children. And because He has recruited us to fight with Him to rescue those caught in the lies of the evil one and proclaim His message of good news, to proclaim freedom to the prisoners, recovery of sight to the blind, and to set the oppressed free.

Discussion, Reflection, and Actionable Suggestions:

1. Have you had questions about why God allows bad things to happen on earth?
2. Adam and Eve's sin caused the fall of man and explains our current situation on earth. Discuss.

3. It was a relief to learn that all the bad that happens on earth is not God's will, but rather, the result of sin, the curse upon the earth, and the works of the devil. Discuss.
4. We need God and God needs us. At God's design, we are partners for taking back the earth for God; He needs our agreement to bring back the will of God on earth. Discuss.

2

Why God Didn't Answer Your Prayer

SECTION TWO IS A collection of stories relating how God reached through the veil to touch my life, (a nobody in the religious world) to prove His passion and favor for me through answering my prayers. However, before we get into that, let's talk about the 14,000-pound elephant in the room. Why didn't God answer your prayer?"

Did you have a good father?

If you didn't, that experience may adversely affect your capacity to understand God. God made fathers to be role models. He intended for them to model the Heavenly Father's love and care.

One of the most significant things Jesus did was to reveal that God is like having a father in heaven. He revealed that God is not just some invisible, uncaring force out there; God is family. He is our Abba[34] Father, and good fathers know what you need and how to love you.

For those who had good fathers, having a father in heaven is a most comforting truth. Nothing is better for a child than to get to know his father and learn how to talk to him. For those who didn't experience a good father, there is still a chance to know the love of a

---

[34] Mark 14:6

father. God made a special promise to you. He said in Psalms[35] that the Lord is a Father to the fatherless. He takes special care of those without good fathers. Begin now to seize the opportunity to experience the love of a father.

Jesus gives us instructions on how to begin our conversation with our Father through "The Lord's Prayer," or "The Model Prayer.[36]" The prayer goes like this: "Our Father, who art in heaven, hallowed be thy name. Thy kingdom come, thy will be done, on earth as it is in heaven. Give us this day our daily bread. And forgive us our trespasses, as we forgive those who trespass against us. And do not lead us into temptation but deliver us from evil. For thine is the kingdom and the power and the glory forever. Amen"

Prayer Changes Things

It is important to note why Jesus gave this prayer. The disciples could have asked Him to teach them anything they wanted. However, they already understood His secret. It was His relationship with God and His prayers.

The disciples marveled at His prayers and how powerful and effective they were. When Jesus prayed, He raised the dead[37], fed 5,000 with little food[38], and healed the sick and disabled. The disciples weren't looking for a powerless prayer they could quote while holding hands in a circle. They wanted their prayers to be powerful and effective. They wanted to get stuff done like Jesus could.

The Lord's Prayer is the prayer Jesus gave them in response. He knew they were asking for power to get things done like He did. He

---

[35] Psalms 68:4-5
[36] Matthew 6:9-13
[37] Luke 8:52-56
[38] John 6:1-14

would not have given them, or us, an ineffective, powerless prayer. Dig deep into it and find its power. We will only begin to scratch the surface here.

Let's look at the first few verses of the prayer Jesus gave.

Our Father who is in heaven. Jesus starts off with relationship. He addresses God as his Father, but not only His, but ours too. He chooses to make Himself our equal as He identifies Himself with us as a child of the Father.

May your name be kept holy. Here we see the love, respect, and honor Jesus has for His Father.

Your kingdom come. Jesus calls for the kingdom of God on earth. He differentiates between the kingdoms of the day and God's kingdom. When we ask for His kingdom to come, we are asking for the restoration of a lost kingdom. Little by little, as His forward agents, we are taking back His kingdom on earth by prayer.

Your will be done. Jesus understands that God's will is good and superior. He trusts God's will and summons it. When we summon His will in faith, then His will comes.

As it is in heaven. This statement reveals to us that God's will is always done in heaven. It also implies that a different situation or environment exists on earth. (Our problems can only be understood by examining what happened to the world when Adam made Satan a consultant for man in the Garden of Eden.)

Jesus establishes that our God is more than the impersonal gods the pagans of that day worshiped. He is a good Father; whose character is worthy of great respect. In His kingdom, His will is good, respected, and followed.

Since Jesus opened this door for us, we can learn of God by looking at the relationship of father and child. Prayer is simply dialogue between a father and his child. Few things are more precious to a father than conversation with his child. Little else can command the attention of a father more than a child's heartfelt request.

As we mature, we begin to understand the relationship is more complicated than merely God is a provider. We learn to appreciate the dynamic between father and child and why some of our prayer requests are beyond the pale of that relationship.

You Will Shoot Your Eye Out

"You will shoot your eye out" is the iconic line from the movie *Christmas Story*. In the movie, Ralphie desperately wants a Red Ryder BB gun. His desire is constantly met with, "You will shoot your eye out," by all the adults in his life.

Ironically, in the movie, it was his father who thought he was ready, but we all understand that a good father also knows when we are not ready.

For me, it was a motorcycle. I desperately wanted a mini-bike motorcycle when I was ten years old. And eventually, my father bought one for me when I was twelve, long after I thought I was ready.

Our Heavenly Father always answers our prayers, but sometimes the answer we get is "no," or at least "not right now." If His answer is "not right now," He knows when we are ready, and His answer will come in due time. The "no" answer is often tough for us to swallow, mostly because we are praying for our will to be done. The Lord's prayer could not be more clear. A powerful prayer God answers "yes" to is the one that is God's will.

Even Jesus endured a "no" answer. Who could forget the prayer in the garden? "Father let this cup pass from me."[39]

---

[39] Matthew 26:39

God, Please Let Mommy and Daddy Get Back Together

Often, we pray that God will intervene in a relationship between two people and fix things. We pray that two people will love each other or that a person we want to love us will love us.

It is not wrong to pray for people who are in a relationship, but our Father is respectful of our choices. We can pray for the Father's will to be done. We can also pray for guidance that circumstances will allow them to better understand the consequences of their actions and attitudes.

However, a father can't make a boy love his daughter or a girl love his son. A father can't make his son's troubled marriage be better. He can advise and counsel, but ultimately, it is up to the two people in the relationship to work out their relationship.

Just Tell Me What to Do

A year or so after college, I was struggling in my career. It seemed like my every decision was the wrong one and my failures were adding up. Feelings of self-pity engulfed me. I went to my father and said, "I am obviously not making good decisions with my life. Please tell me what to do."

My father said, "I can't tell you what to do. This is your life. I am here for you, but you have to figure it out for yourself." In the moment, that was not what I wanted to hear, but in hindsight, that was the wise advice. If he had tried to figure it out for me, and it didn't work out, then I would have him to blame instead of taking responsibility for my own decisions.

There have been other times of desperation when I went to the Lord with the same request: "Lord, just tell me what to do. Please tell me and I will do it." The Lord, being a wise Father, didn't tell me either. Instead, He trained me with difficult lessons and hard work. The training involved stepping out into unknown territory by faith. Some of the paths took me down dead-end roads to learn lessons about wrong roads.

Additional training involved getting more education to make myself more valuable and working more hours to increase my offering of services to others. At times, it felt like He was testing my persistence. There have been times when no answer from God caused me to pause and examine my life. Did I have sinful actions and attitudes causing God to resist me and my prayers to get my attention?[40]

Being a good father is a difficult and complicated job while your child is suffering. This is especially true when a father knows his child is counting on a "yes" answer and the answer is "no."

Living with Your Decisions

The answer to some prayers require our agreement. It is surprising that arranged marriages ever work out, but some do. However, few Westerners believe this is the best way. I don't believe God arranges marriages. Neither is it very wise to marry without your parents' blessing. There are exceptions to everything, but the believing father (and mother) should act as a source of wisdom and counsel during momentous decisions.

In the same way, the Lord wants to provide wisdom and counsel to us, while leaving the final decision in our hands. He knows we get swept up by our emotions and need a steady hand and a strong shoulder to lean on. He provides that to us if we seek His counsel. But ultimately, He understands that we must learn to live with our own decisions.

Even if the Lord orchestrates an excellent opportunity for us, it doesn't mean He forces us to act. There are countless opportunities the

---

[40] Psalms 66:18

Lord orchestrates for people. He orchestrates opportunities for relationships, relocations, education, jobs, etc., but the person requesting may decide against moving forward for a myriad of reasons. Like any good father, He knows that with any decision, there are consequences, and He respects our decision to avoid certain situations, even ones He helped orchestrate.

Why We Didn't Act

So, why didn't you act when the opportunity presented itself?

Maybe you were afraid, afraid to take a leap of faith. Perhaps you were afraid of failure or losing what you would leave behind. Possibly, you were afraid of intimacy or responsibility. Maybe, out of stubbornness, you rejected an opportunity that presented itself because it wasn't perfect enough. Conceivably, the opportunity passed you by because you were not ready. Perhaps you changed your mind and decided that is not what you wanted.

Whatever the reason, it is likely time to stop blaming God and feeling self-pity and "**own**" your situation. Take ownership that you are where you are, in large part, due to your own actions and decisions. It is not God's fault.

It is the same with career opportunities. We may contend that God did not give us the career break we prayed for. How many opportunities presented themselves, but we decided to turn down because we thought it was not for us? Maybe we thought it was beneath us, but we didn't know the potential behind the opportunity the Lord was making available. Oh, the mystery of the road not taken.

When we blame God because we are alone, is it because the opportunity never presented or because we decided against a marriage? Who is to say the decision not to marry was not a good one? There are no perfect people and no relationship will be devoid of conflict and heartbreak. If we look long and hard enough, flaws are bound to surface. Though marriage is a blessing, it also has obligations to be considered.

God Has Given You Almost Everything You Ever Asked For

My dad once said to me, "God has given you almost everything that you have ever prayed for."

I asked, "How would you know that?"

"I know what you pray for."

"You do?" I asked.

"Sure. And I know you have received almost everything."

It blew me away that my dad knew me well enough to know my prayer requests. Equally, it surprised me that he was attentive enough to know I have received almost everything I ever prayed for or wanted.

His statement was qualified with "almost," but still, receiving almost everything is quite amazing.

However, there was a time when I was angry at God. I blamed him that everything had not worked out as I envisioned. I wailed and shook my fist at God, reminiscent of Lieutenant Dan in the movie *Forrest Gump*. It was easy for me to relate to Lieutenant Dan calling for a lightning strike as he hung from the mast of the boat.

This week, I visited a new friend Donnie at his home. He has three children, with his youngest son Mac being about four years old. Mac was irritated for some reason. His sisters were taking a tennis lesson, and no one was paying attention to Mac. He had a couple of attention-seeking outbursts during the lesson that went ignored. After the lesson, Donnie was showing me around his property when Mac screamed out, "I hate you!" Looking over to see the little boy's contorted expression, I thought, "That kid really wants his daddy's attention." Donnie smiled and said, "We don't talk like that around here, son."

It is easy to see myself in Mac. Why doesn't God simply give me what I ask for? Wouldn't it be easier for the all-powerful God to grant my request, rather than watch me pout? My unanswered prayer has more to do with my own character deficiencies. After many years, it is still too raw to discuss openly, though you will no doubt see glimpses in future chapters that will indicate what it is. This one "no" I received may have shaped me and my faith more than all the "yeses." It shook me from my pedestal. It humbled me and made me a better and more compassionate person.

The more I understand the predicament of the world since Eden and how God is a father, the more I understand things are not so simple. It is not simple at all when you understand how our Father gives us a will of our own and chooses not to interfere. Many of my prayers require my acceptance of risk with the opportunities. His answers require a decision from me. I must take responsibility and ownership.

Often what we call unanswered prayer, or God's withholding, is actually us withholding from ourselves. We make decisions not to love or risk because of past hurts. We make vows to ourselves and self-proclamations never to put ourselves in that position again. We harden our hearts and tie God's hands.

Withholding from ourselves what we need due to fear or lack of faith can be just as painful. But it is our issue and not God's. We begin to find hope when we take ownership of our issues. Things can change when we take ownership and responsibility.

Things change when we begin to behave differently. One of my favorite sayings is, "We must behave ourselves out of what we behaved ourselves into." Life can totally change in an area of our life based on a single decision to act. The Lord is passionately for us and wants to help us, but some things he has left up to us.

Discussion, Reflection and Actionable Suggestions:

1. Do you need to stop blaming God that some of your desires have gone unmet?
2. Have you been withholding from yourself? Have you made vows or self-proclamations that tie the hands of God? Consider this prayer: Lord, please forgive me for blaming you for unmet needs. I renounce any ungodly vow or proclamation that is tying your hands. Please reveal to me what I am withholding from myself. In Jesus' Name.
3. Are you willing to own your own circumstances and ask the Lord to give you the wisdom and courage to make a decision and then act on it? Consider this prayer: Lord, help me to own my own circumstances. Help me to take responsibility for my own decisions. Please give me wisdom in the future to make wiser decisions. In Jesus' Name.
4. Do you need to go back to the Lord and apologize to Him for your actions and attitudes toward Him? Consider this prayer: Lord, please forgive me for my wrong attitudes, words, and actions toward you. I have been wrong. In Jesus' Name.
5. Do you need to humble yourself and praise and thank Him for all the wonderful things He has done for you?
6. Is there a decision you need to make that is holding back God's will for your life?

3

What Are You Praying For?

How Praying Together Can Strengthen a Relationship

AS I SAID IN THE LAST chapter, my dad once said to me, "God has given you almost everything you have asked for."

"How do you know that?" I asked.

"I am your father. I know what you are praying for."

That brief conversation changed me and my relationship with my father. "Am I that transparent?" I wondered, "or was it just my father who could see because of his sensitivity to me and my desires?"

My relationship with my father deepened that day. I realized he knew my deepest desires and he had seen prayers answered. That must have been an indelible moment for him and a boost to his own faith. All this made him special to me on a new level, because he was now a part of my secret life of prayer.

The conversation with my dad helped me realize something. If I can know you deeply enough that I know what you are praying about, then the quality of our relationship increases. Who doesn't want more quality relationships?

What Are You Praying For?

So why not simply ask those we love about the content of their prayers? And if they trust us, they will tell us. If they won't, or can't tell us, which is quite understandable, we learn something about them. We learn they are praying for something very personal. It may even include us. Even knowing that increases our intimacy and may motivate us to pray for them.

And if they tell us what they are praying for, several good things can happen. First, we can agree with them in their prayer. Jesus made this profound statement:

> *Again, truly, if two of you on earth agree about anything they ask for, it will be done for them by my Father in heaven (Matthew 18:19).*

Obviously, the thing we agree on must be in keeping God's will, but what an astounding promise this is!

Secondly, in addition to coming into agreement, we also learn how to encourage. For example, if a friend is praying for his alcoholic father to get help, then we know how to encourage our friend. Having this knowledge can also help us be more compassionate and understanding.

Helping Our Children Develop Spiritually

Asking our children spiritual questions helps in their spiritual development. It helps them to tap into their spiritual nature and to look and listen for God in the still, small voice that is calling their name and beckoning them to enter in.

This is easy for children. Jesus said, "You must become like a little child to enter into the Kingdom of God."[41] Children have an advantage over adults when it comes to faith and the imagination to feel and see

---

[41] Matthew 18:3

God. I use imagination in the best way here, for it is God who gave imagination to help us find Him. The earlier we find Him and the more our finding Him is validated by those we trust, the more that relationship shapes and transforms us.

It is pure enjoyment for me to ask children spiritual questions. The conversations are often memorable, and I love making connections with children. One of my favorite questions to ask is, "What is the Lord teaching you?" This question can spark hours of conversation and was the inspiration for the question, "What are you praying for?" And yes, it is possible to have a spiritual conversation with a seven-year-old, and even a teenager.

It will always stand out in my memory the first time I asked Chandler, age nine, what he was praying for. The impact of the question was obvious by the ensuing conversation. There is no other way I could have known the burdens a little boy carried for his wayward father or been able to offer perspective without knowing what he was praying for.

A Difficult Question

No doubt, this question can be a little difficult at first, since most Americans don't have spiritual conversations with anyone. Our culture has told us that faith and spirituality are private matters. Whoever deemed this so didn't find the idea in the Bible. To the contrary, the Bible models and gives instruction to share our faith and build up faith in our communities.[42]

Surveys tell us that most Americans don't attend church regularly,[43] but the majority pray for help with problems.[44] Doesn't the benefit of

---

[42] Matthew 28:19
[43] http://news.gallup.com/poll/166613/four-report-attending-church-last-week.aspx

asking the question outweigh the discomfort? Isn't this especially true if it deepens a relationship or opens a conversation that leads someone to the true source of help and potentially their true destiny of being a partner with God?

This conversation can strengthen our relationships, our faith, and even our spiritual IQ, as together, we delve deeper into this love relationship with the Heavenly Father.

Epilogue

Stella is a friend who is part of my fellowship group. After reviewing this material one evening with the group, it led her to ask the following question:

Stella: I am not so bold as to ask someone about their prayer life or relationship with the Lord. Do you think the Lord is displeased with me that I can't lead people to the Lord?

Clay: Well, I think you can lead people to the Lord. Anytime someone comes to you with a problem they can't solve, you can lead them to the Lord. Isn't He the one you turn to when you have nowhere else to turn?

Stella: I never thought of it like that before. That sounds easy.

Clay: I think it can be that easy. For me, the more I truly believe He is the solution people are looking for to satisfy their deepest needs, the easier it is to recommend Him.

Discussion, Reflection, and Actionable Suggestions:

1. Is there someone in your life that knows what you are praying for? If not, consider this prayer: Lord, please deepen an existing

---

[44] http://www.pewresearch.org/fact-tank/2016/05/04/5-facts-about-prayer/

relationship or send someone into my life that I trust enough to share my prayers. In Jesus' Name.
2. Have you witnessed the power of agreement? If so, discuss what you have witnessed.
3. Is there a child in your life that you can help wake up to their spiritual side?

4

What Prayers Has God Answered For You?

The effective prayer of a righteous man can accomplish much.
--James 5:16

A GROUP OF SEASONED Christians should have lots of stories to tell about answered prayer, right?

A year or so ago our education director asked me to lead a discussion group on prayer. The group was mostly mature adults at the church I attend. I began with the following statement:

> *"There is a connection between faith and answered prayer.[45][46] If we will share our stories of answered prayer with each other, it will build our faith in prayer. If we can increase our faith in prayer, the more prayers we will see answered. One builds on the other."*

I felt proud of myself for coming up with such an inventive and compelling premise. Then we kicked off the discussion with a simple statement: "During this series of lessons on prayer, I would like for each of us to share a story of answered prayer. Now, who would like to go first?"

---

[45] Matthew 21:22
[46] Mark 11:24

There was a stunned silence. Let's give it time, I thought. So we waited until the silence was getting to be uncomfortable. Still nothing, and no one showed any body language suggesting something was coming to mind.

These people were not shrinking violets. Either no one had a compelling story of answered prayer, or if they had, they couldn't remember one when put on the spot. Either way, the testimony of answered prayer was not on the tip of the tongue.

The Reason for This Book

The next day I decided to write this book recounting answered prayer in my own life. My hope is to ignite a discussion and bring greater awareness of the Lord's answers to our prayers. We all need the encouragement answered prayer gives. The following chapters are a compilation of my faith-shaping stories of answered prayers, proving God hears and answers. When God didn't answer my prayers as I had hoped, I share how those prayers shaped my faith too.

Included are my stories of answers to a child's prayer, mercy to a junior high football player, and relief for a sexually-abused teen. There are accounts of miraculous healing, angel visitations, matchmaking, overcoming paralyzing fears, and facing death. Finally, there are confounding events orchestrated in ways that make it difficult to deny there was a guiding hand.

The culmination of the stories proves, once again, that our prayers are heard and answered by the Lord.[47] More importantly, they are effective for the work the Lord is doing. They are also convincing that a part of the purpose for our prayers, and our wrestling with them, is to fashion us into who we are.

---

[47] I John 5:14-15

We Have an Enemy

Equally important is to acknowledge we have an enemy. His primary mission is to cast doubt on our faith. He hopes to steal our future, kill our faith, and destroy our will to do the good work the Lord created us to accomplish.[48] Jesus called our enemy a murderer, a liar, and the father of lies.[49] He is, no doubt, a formidable opponent. Prayer can be the great equalizer in our battle against him.

This process of prayer, hearing and witnessing answers, contributes to building our faith and transforming us into a person God saves for His family. My purpose for sharing the following stories is to bolster your faith in a good God who hears, loves passionately, and responds.

May the Lord bless you with greater faith as you read these stories of answered prayer.

Discussion, Reflection, and Actionable Suggestions:

1. Do you have a story of answered prayer on the tip of your tongue?
2. "There is a connection between faith and answered prayer. If we will share our stories of answered prayers with each other, it will build our faith in prayer. If we can increase our faith in prayer, the more prayers we will see answered. One builds on the other." Discuss the author's premise.
3. Part of the purpose for our prayers is to fashion us into who we are. How do you think prayer has shaped you?

---

[48] John 10:10
[49] John 8:44

5

Why You Don't Have What You Want

But when you pray, go into your room, close the door and pray to your Father, who is unseen. Then your Father, who sees what is done in secret, will reward you.

--Matthew 6:6

"MOM AND DAD ALWAYS give me more than they do you," I said to my brother Gary when I was fourteen. "Do you ever wonder why that is?"

"Not really."

"Well, it is because I ask for things. You never ask for things."

"I don't want to ask. I want to get things on my own."

"Good for you, but I am going to keep asking," I said.

What Do You Want?

The brother of Jesus composed a letter that has been preserved. In it, he wrote to other Jewish brothers concerning their heavenly Father:

> *You do not have what you want because you do not ask (James 4:2).*

Could it be that simple? Of course not. We are not just asking anyone. We are asking our Father who knows what we need before we need it and what we want when we don't even realize what we want.

James goes on to talk about why we don't get what we ask for, and most of our focus and energy goes to that portion of the verse. You might want to reread Chapter 1, *Why God Didn't Answer Your Prayer*. However, I want to focus on the first part of the verse:

> *You do not have what you want because you do not ask (James 4:2).*

This problem should be easy to alleviate. We simply spend more time asking -- not demanding -- but asking for our wants and needs to be met. We end our prayers just as Jesus did, with "not our will, but Yours be done."[50]

In the following verse, Jesus gives us great insight into the secret of His success and what He believes is available to us:

> *When you pray, go into your room, close the door and pray to your Father, who is unseen. Then your Father, who sees what is done in secret, will reward you (Matthew 6:6).*

Asking

I have asked for a lot. The Lord has answered thousands of specific prayers for me. Hundreds of times I prayed for a sick person who got well. I asked for people to find jobs, and they found them. Expecting parents ask me to pray for a baby in the womb and the baby was born healthy. There were prayers for relationships to get better and they did. The parent of a rebellious child asked for prayer, and the child lived through it. I've asked for encouragement, and someone called or

---

[50] Luke 22:42

came by. I prayed the Lord would comfort a friend during times of grief, and they were.

A lot of prayers came true. Unfortunately, it seems like the attribution to God is sometimes quickly forgotten.

I don't always get what I ask for, of course. We just buried a friend many of us have been praying for diligently. Too many I prayed for still ended in divorce. Some kids got worse before they got better. Some friends got answers, but not exactly what they wanted. For others, the answer felt like too long to wait. One man confided, with angst, that after years of praying for an outcome, "If God were to answer 'yes' now, I am not really sure I still want it."

The Little Things

I should be a very spiritual person because of my constant prayers to find things I misplaced. My number one most frequent prayer is not for world peace, but for help finding my car keys. It is amazing how many times I have been frantic about running late and unable to find my keys. Sometimes I say to myself, "You can't find them, and the Lord knows where they are. Why not stop and ask Him?"

I can't tell you I found them immediately every time after praying, but it is amazing how many times, after praying, I found them almost immediately. Sometimes, it is as simple as remembering to look where I had them last. But I have been motivated to look in places where I would never look, like the time I dropped them in the yard.

But even when God delays his answer in finding my keys, who's to say He didn't have His reasons. Maybe He was protecting me against a scheme of the devil, or as the Lord's Prayer puts it, He was delivering me from evil.

It may sound silly to some, but it is important to me to keep Him in my consciousness and internal conversations and not just bring Him in for the big stuff. For me, it is about relationship, and that includes the mundane.

The Lord has answered all my requests. Sometimes He said no. There has been an obvious connection between my prayers and what has happened around me. He shows His great desire for me to know Him when He responds to my prayers, and I will never underestimate the reward He gives to those who go into their room and secretly spend time with Him.

Discussion, Reflection, and Actionable Suggestions:

1. Do you talk to God? If so, do you talk to Him about whatever concerns you or only the big stuff?
2. Do you give God credit or think it was a lucky coincidence when you get an answer to prayer?
3. Do you have alone time with God to talk and listen?
4. Do you need a little more confidence and faith that God really hears and answers your prayers? If so, consider this prayer: Father, as we go through this book and study, will you help me to have eyes to see and ears to hear you in my world and my circumstances. Help me in my unbelief to, once again, believe you love me, hear me, and answer. In Jesus' Name.

I am not the pastor of a big church. Neither am I a priest, prophet, preacher, elder, or deacon. I didn't graduate with a seminary degree or go to a Christian school. In the religious world I am a nobody. If God will hear and answer the prayers of a nobody, then He will hear and answer your prayers too.

Section II: Answered Prayers of a Nobody

6

Now I Lay Me Down to Sleep

Truly, I say to you, unless you turn and become like children, you will never enter the Kingdom of Heaven.

-- Matthew 18:3

I HAVE BEEN IN ONE KNIFE FIGHT. At age nine my older brother Gary slapped me "upside the head" in front of a couple of his friends for using his bed like a trampoline. Ego wounded, I retrieved the butcher knife to get revenge. As we wrestled, he pulled the blade through my hand, cutting two fingers to the bone. Scared, we bandaged the fingers and never told my parents until years later.

Like most of us, my life has had its conflicts. We live in a dangerous world. I faced my share of bullies, both at home and away. A few times I cowered in fear, and there were times I was the bully. To think our prayers can insulate us from conflicts would be naive. To say God uses conflict would be more accurate. Gary and I shared a room and bunk beds until I was seven and he was thirteen. I now sympathize that he had to share a room with me until he was a teenager. The inevitable conflict shaped me too.

There were advantages to sharing a room with an older brother. For one, I never had to sleep in a dark room by myself. I usually had to go to bed first, and each night started out being alone. I did have my companions with me for comfort. There was a stuffed version of our school mascot, Leo the Lion, and Snoopy, with his Red Baron glasses and scarf. There was Mitch, a crocheted green snake, and El, a six-foot-long brown snake my brother Elwyn won tossing rings at the carnival.

Each night before Mother left my room, I asked her to leave the door open. I wanted the comfort of feeling connected, and I knew as soon as Gary came to bed, the door was closing. After that, all there was to cling to was the tiny sliver of light shining through the bottom crack.

Teaching Me to Pray

When Mother tucked me in, she spent time sitting on the side of my bed. It was as much a ritual for her as it was for me. The day wasn't complete without her watching over my prayers.

My mother taught me how to pray. I will never forget the prayer I said:

Now I lay me down to sleep.
I pray the Lord my soul to keep.
If I should die before I wake,
I pray the Lord my soul to take.
God bless Mother and Daddy, Joel and Wadene, Tamara, Brent and Angie. Bless Jeanette and Jimmy, Susie, Jenny and Jimmy Lee. Bless Elwyn and Nancy, Heidi, Judy and Melanie, and bless Gary. And Father, please end the war in Vietnam.
In Jesus' Name, Amen.

No doubt the prayer varied somewhat from time to time, but the memory exists of praying it over and over...night after night...year after year. Was that a meaningless child's prayer, or was it a prayer that reached the very ears of the Almighty?

How It Turned Out

The war in Vietnam finally ended when I was fourteen. It felt odd when it was over, since it had gone on my whole life.

All my family members have lived blessed lives, though not without pain and struggle. My mother, who died in 1982 after a battle with colon cancer, was blessed. She did what she loved both as a mother and later with a career.

My father died in 2003 after marrying twice more. He lost his second wife, Merita, after surgery to repair a valve in her heart in 1989. Anna came along in 1995, until his death. He lived to see 11 grandchildren and 21 great grandchildren. Life as a WWII veteran, a businessman, and a farmer were all part of his experience. He was a leader, speaker, and elder in his church for over 40 years. He loved learning, teaching, and gardening, and all this he had an opportunity to do.

My brothers and sister have had their ups and downs, gains and losses. There have been good times and lean times as they navigated with careers in oil exploration, manufacturing, civil service, and human resources. My siblings live as blessed people by all comparative measures.

There has been marriage, children, and grandchildren…good times and bad, adventure and living the daily routine. There has been divorce, family separation and estrangement, heartache, resentment, anger and depression, sickness, tragedy and death. And yes, there have been feelings of abandonment from God.

My brothers and sister have all lived to see their own children live productive lives. Of course, their lives are a mixed bag of ups and downs too. And not to minimize the significance of their battle scars, by human standards they are blessed.

Did the Lord Answer the Prayers of a Little Boy?

Has the Lord answered the consistent and persistent prayers of a little boy for blessings on his family? Of course, some answers are still ongoing, but in retrospect, I believe He has.

What does being blessed mean? Is it being successful in all your endeavors? Does it mean being financially successful and without material need? Is it having your family together, happy and healthy? All of these are wonderful blessings, no doubt.

However, could you still be blessed even if the opposites are true? Could you be physically sick, in need of material things, in a broken home, and still be blessed? If this life is temporary and there awaits for the one connected to God a new, more beautiful life, then that connection is the ultimate blessing. With it comes a great hope and future.

As a boy I didn't know what I was asking for, but I think I do now. For my family to be materially rich but poor in relationship to the Lord would be a curse. Being without a want could be the worst thing that ever happens to us. It might blind us to the need to seek a relationship with God. Our tragedy and misfortunes could be regarded as a curse or just the thing that put us in the frame of mind to seek a relationship with the Lord.

Being Truly Blessed

A life orchestrated to come face to face with the Lord and accepting His offer is a better definition of blessed. Being in relationship with Jesus is being blessed.[51]

Inside, there still exists the little boy whose mother sat on the side of his bed teaching him to pray. God continues to answer the prayers

---

[51] John 3:16

of a little boy to bless his family. As I contemplate what the afterlife will be like, I hope it includes the Lord sharing how He interceded in our lives and answered our prayers.

Epilogue

Sometime after writing this chapter I decided to re-institute this practice of calling out the names of my family members and asking for God's will and blessing in their lives. What I didn't anticipate was how blessed it made me feel to be intertwined with so many lives. It induced a new sense of connectedness that has added a layer of richness to my day.

N.T. Wright, the Anglican theologian, said, "Your prayers will outlive your life." What better way to invest your time than to call forth the will of a good Father for those you love.

Discussion, Reflection, and Actionable Suggestions:

1. Can you think of a conflict that shaped your life?
2. Are you teaching the children in your life to pray?
3. The author suggests that you could lack in outward blessings, yet still be blessed with the ultimate blessing of being in relationship with God. Discuss this suggestion.
4. Are you demonstrating at home that a relationship with Jesus is the most important thing in this life?

7

When You Want to Quit

For the moment, all discipline seems painful rather than pleasant, but later it yields the peaceful fruit of righteousness to those who have been trained by it.
-- Hebrews 12:11

"HELP ME LORD," I cried out. "I can't take this anymore. It is not worth it." My cry was for mercy, though I didn't realize it. I am astounded how He came through.

The Lord is Intent on Building a Person of Character

The Lord is in the character-building business. Character is built through discipline. Discipline is hard.

The word *disciple* is a derivative of the word *discipline*. To be a disciple is to follow in the disciplines of a master. Jesus disciplined His followers in what they would later call "The Way" of their master.

A martial arts student may give us a better picture of a disciple than does the typical church member. Breaking boards and self-defense is only a small piece of what martial arts is about. Martial arts training is about discipline. The martial artist learns to practice disciplined thinking and conduct according to his art.

I like the martial arts analogy as it relates to Christian disciples. The word *martial* means "as appropriate for war," and according to the Bible, the Christian is in the midst of a war. However, it seems that many Christian disciples have deviated from seeing ourselves as disciplined warriors. We are failing to recognize an enemy, a battle, or the need for discipline.

According to the Apostle Paul, we do this at our own peril. He tells us to put on the whole armor of God.[52] He warns to stay mindful of the spiritual battle that rages around us.

The Discipline of "The Way"

Jesus is our master and teaches us the disciplines of *His way*. Before being called Christians, the early disciples called themselves followers of "The Way." This title has a mystical martial arts ring to it that I like.

There are several disciplines the master Jesus puts before the disciple to master. As students, we practice self-control, like controlling the tongue, our sexuality, and our emotions. Then there are disciplines we practice like prayer, giving, and fasting. And finally, we grow in attitudes of the heart such as compassion, grace, and mercy.

These are all difficult. To fail in these disciplines is to miss the mark. Apostle Paul wrote much about the disciplines. He elaborated on his frustration. Paul said, "For I do not understand my own actions. For I do not do what I want, but I do the very thing I hate. For my very nature is to be undisciplined and to fall short of the standard. O wretched man that I am."[53] The disciplines of the Lord are hard.

God Used Discipline to Develop Character in His Chosen People Israel

---

[52] Ephesians 6:10-20
[53] Romans 7:14-25

God could choose any way He wished to teach His children character. He often chose what was hard.

> *My son, do not despise the Lord's discipline or be weary of his reproof, for the Lord reproves him whom he loves, as a father the son in whom he delights (Proverbs 3:11-12).*

During Israel's infancy as a people, the Lord used slavery lasting hundreds of years to shape and prepare them. Even as He sent Moses to rescue them, He allowed Pharaoh to increase their workload and make life more difficult.[54]

To add to their discipline, following their rescue God gave them laws. These laws were simple and straightforward, but they were hard.[55] The people could not keep them. The discipline required wasn't in their nature.

As if that were not enough hardship to condition them, the Lord chose another forty years in the wilderness. There, the people were without permanent homes, no suitable soil for growing crops or grazing, and sparse water supplies. He made it super hard. At times, too hard, to the point they cried out for fear of death.

Twice, they were without water in the desert wilderness.[56] A human cannot live without water longer than three days. The people cried out.

The Lord is no fool. He knew they needed water. He also knew they needed something more than they needed water. They needed to know He was real. They needed to know He could hear them. And they needed to know that He cared about them.

Out of a rock, the Lord chose to show His mercy and grace by bringing out enough water to satisfy the whole camp. Discipline builds

---

[54] Exodus 5:5-8
[55] Exodus 20
[56] Exodus 17:1-7

character, but mercy and grace shows compassion and love. Compassion and love build a relationship.

God Uses Others to Build Our Character

God is still in the character-building business. He is still providing hard places for people to learn discipline.

The Lord used football to shape my early life. It taught me difficult, but valuable lessons.

Football's ability to build character is one of the chief reasons Americans love the sport. A Russian general once remarked, "Americans have a military advantage over Russians." When asked what he meant, he remarked, "It is the military training American boys receive playing football."

When I was in the eighth grade, my constant companion was Tim Gravitt. He was the best athlete in our school, and not only my friend, but he was my competition. We competed at everything and for everything. The first thing he did when he moved to town in the fourth grade was take my girlfriend. He also was the champion on the playground and the person you didn't want to fistfight.

Tim and I were inseparable, but everyone knew he was the alpha dog. We wore out the grass in the backyard playing baseball, basketball, and football. We also played ping-pong, Monopoly, Rook, and anything else we could think of. He was always pushing me to be better.

The spring of our eighth-grade year was our second year of organized football. Tim was a few pounds heavier, but we were close to the same size. He was my tackling partner and would one day play linebacker in college at 6 feet and 225 pounds.

We Will Experience Spiritual Warfare

It seemed to us the coaches designed our junior high football drills to toughen us up, weed us out, and call into question our fledgling manhood. It was hard and painful, and there was no easy way out. You had to tough it out or quit.

Tough it out or quit is the recipe for spiritual warfare. It makes for an agonizing decision. Who would I be without this long-held dream of playing for my school?

The devil is watching for us to get discouraged, and when we are, he attacks with temptations to complain, grumble, blame, and quit.[57] I know that has happened to you too, because it is common to us all at one time or another.

The Way is Hard

Like His children of Israel, I believe He orchestrates hard things to happen in our lives. He disciplined them, and He disciplines us. He presents us with situations that require more than we can handle so we will look for help and cry for mercy. We see this insight from the book of Numbers. The Israelites had set out on their journey to the promised land. We get a glimpse of their attitude:

> *And they journeyed from Mount Hor by the way of the Red Sea, to compass the land of Edom; and the soul of the people was much discouraged because of the way (Numbers 21:4).*

Isn't that the most natural thing? We become discouraged because of the way. It is hard, painful, and uncomfortable. We get discouraged and we want to quit.

---

[57] Matthew 4:1

My eighth-grade year was in the days prior to the new football helmet technology. The older hand-me-downs that we used had a canvas suspension interior, and if you were lucky, you got one that fit.

Many of my teammates will never forget the day we looked over at Michael Dickinson and saw blood streaming down his face. It was bad. Sort of looked like a protagonist in a horror movie with a bloody face, looking back underneath the caged facemask. Finally, I said, "Michael, what happened to you?" And Coach Lyons looked over, trying not to seem alarmed.

Michael said, "I don't know, I hit Charlie real hard, but now my head's killing me." Coach said, "Take your helmet off and let's take a look." He tried to take his helmet off and let out a huge groan. "I can't," he said. "Something is sticking in my forehead." Finally, the coach had the manager fetch a screwdriver to back out a couple of wrong-sized screws used to attach the facemask. The screws had literally bored into poor Michael's forehead.

I Wanted to Quit

The tackling technique in those days was for both tackler and runner to run full speed through the other man, head-first, crown of helmet to crown of helmet. In spring training that year, we had a group session every day, where we would spend thirty minutes or so practicing this battering-ram technique over and over.

Tim, the future collegiate linebacker, was my partner. After our first practice, I had a persistent headache most of the time. I also taught myself a technique for giving my neck a chiropractic adjustment to relieve some stiffness. I used this technique several times a day on into adulthood. It wasn't until Chapter 27 that I received permanent relief.

Many of my friends quit the team to get out of this thirty-minute session. There is a stigma associated with quitting the football team in my small town. Most of us had known others who had quit and were labeled *quitter*. My high school even had a slogan that went, "A quitter never wins and a winner never quits." *Quitter* was not a title you wanted attached to you.

During that spring, the eighth-graders on our team went from about thirty players to fifteen. I dreaded every day because I knew I had to go to practice and crack helmets with Tim Gravitt. I was always looking for an opportunity to switch partners when possible.

Thoughts of quitting the team were becoming ever-present as a way of avoiding this thirty-minute session. I was working up my courage and steeling myself to the humiliation of quitting. I sat in the bathtub, transfixed on the faucet's drip, drip, drip, and splash in the pool below. I saw myself telling my brothers and friends about quitting the team before I blurted out, "Help me, Lord. I can't take this anymore. It is not worth it." I didn't realize I was praying for mercy from the discipline. I didn't know what He could do, but I prayed for help. I thought I was asking Him to help me work up the courage to quit the next day.

The Lord Has Mercy on Us

It just so happened that another local high school scheduled my dad as the emcee for their football banquet that night, and he asked me to go along. The speaker for the banquet was none other than Pat Sullivan, the Auburn University quarterback destined that fall to win the Heisman Trophy.

Before Pat's speech, my dad introduced me to him as a fellow quarterback, and I asked for his autograph. Dad had no idea I was planning to quit the next day. I felt the pressure of disappointing him.

Pat was a great young speaker who talked of his faith and his love for football. I desperately needed to hear a message of faith at that moment.

That night, I decided to give football one more day. The next day at practice, when we normally broke into groups for tackling drills, the coach said, "Mize, today I want you to go with Coach Lyons to work on your footwork."

I couldn't believe it. While the rest of the guys were lining up cracking skulls, I was working on footwork. Wow, what wonderful news! The coaches did not ask me to participate in tackling drills for the remaining two weeks of practice, and each day I gladly worked on my footwork drills and secretly felt sorry for everyone else.

I couldn't help but feel like the Lord intervened for me. He had mercy on me. Not only did He relieve me from head-on tackling drills, but He sent college football's number one player to encourage me not to quit. And I still have Pat's autograph all these years later. It reminds me of God's mercy toward me.

A Spiritual Battle

For every young man and woman, there is a spiritual battle going on. The devil tried to discourage me. He tried to get me to quit. I still remember the thoughts in the tub, "I can't take this anymore. It is not worth it." That is what the devil whispers in our ear when *the way is too hard*. He whispers, "You have to do something. Take the easy road." And I think I would have quit had I continued the tackling drill.

That is not the only thing I ever wanted to quit. It is not even the only time I wanted to quit football. There have been less than happy endings with other endeavors where I did give up and quit. Either I didn't have what it took or was not willing to persevere. It didn't prove to be the end of the world for me, and there have been second chances, and third and fourth. The Lord never wastes experiences. We can always learn, and even when we can't help ourselves, our experience can help others.

I know people face a lot of very hard things. They face hard marriages, hard-to-deal-with teens, hard jobs, hard physical conditions, addictions, and hard financial situations. The spiritual warfare going on inside us tempts us with the easy way or easy fix.

Jesus dealt with spiritual warfare in the Garden of Gethsemane. The way He had to go was too hard. As a man, He wanted an easier way. Thankfully, for us, He stayed the course and endured the hard way. Death was His only mercy. We are all blessed because of His great love and that decision.

Many of my teammates quit football that spring, but my five best friends did not quit, even without the mercy I received. They may have been contemplating quitting too. By staying the course, did we influence each other? Had one of us quit, how would that have influenced us? Are you discouraged because *the way* is hard? Do you want to quit?

Epilogue One

Unfortunately, for our football team, I didn't get much bigger as I got older. My abilities were best summed up by one of our assistant coaches, Rip Harmon. He said, "Mize, you play for us because you have intangibles." "What does that mean, Coach?" I asked. "That means you play for us because you have something besides skills." "Thanks, Coach, that makes me feel better," I said.

During the second game of my junior year, I suffered a triple fracture of my left leg that preceded a difficult recovery. Tim Gravitt, who was still the best athlete on the team, took over my duties as quarterback. He was bigger, stronger, and faster than me. Going into our senior year, he now had more experience as a varsity quarterback than I did.

However, during my senior year, the coaches moved us back to our old positions. We had a glorious, memory-filled season. We won ten games and were the region champions, going on to the playoffs.

The five I considered my best friends in the eighth grade stayed together and made it to our senior season. It was no surprise the team voted Tim Gravitt as Most Valuable Player, Johnny Frazier as Best Defensive Player, and Mark Bates received the Earl Frank Walker Award, an award for citizenship and all-around contribution to the team. Two others, of those original five, were Donnie Aderholt, who beat me out as a sophomore to start at cornerback and Mac McAlpine, a two-way starter on offense and defense.

As Coach Harmon reminded me, my skills were marginal, but I will always appreciate my teammates honoring me along with Johnny Frazier, as a team captain; along with the award of Co Best Offensive Player, alongside Mark Townsend. This was my teammates being charitable toward me, since Mark was a two-time All-State running back. None of the high school glory or memories could have happened had the Lord not seen me through when the way was *too hard*.

Epilogue Two

On two occasions, my old high school contacted me to be the keynote speaker for their annual football banquet. The keynote speaker is usually reserved for a famous college or professional athlete or coach. I have no significant reputation as a keynote speaker, and I have no idea why they would ask me to be their speaker. However, I felt honored. I choose to believe the Lord works in the hearts of people to do favors for those He loves.

Discussion, Reflection, and Actionable Suggestions:

1. Do you think Christianity has lost its identity as a people practicing a discipline?
2. Do the Lord's requirements for discipline seem too hard at times?
3. Can you see that the Lord has used difficult things in your life to discipline you and build your character?
4. Are you aware of the spiritual struggle when the way is hard and you want to quit?
5. Do you turn to the Lord when the way gets hard? Do you cry out for mercy?
6. Has God given you a second chance -- or third -- or fourth?
7. Is He giving you the grace to hang on for one more day?
8. Can you allow the pain and struggle to build something good in you?

8

Forgiveness is Given but Trust is Earned

And whenever you stand praying, forgive, if you have anything against anyone, so that your Father also who is in heaven may forgive you your trespasses.
-- Mark 11:25

AT AGE FIFTEEN I BECAME the victim of a shameful act. The act against me triggered tormenting thoughts. It took from me a portion of the years that were supposed to be carefree. Answered prayer led me back to a place of freedom.

Getting to Forgiveness

In most areas of life, we are acutely aware of the consequences of our blunders. In football, we call the consequences a *penalty*; while driving, it is called a *fine*; in court, a *sentence*; and in the spiritual realm, we call it *restitution*.

Jesus said, "And whenever you stand praying, forgive, if you have anything against anyone, so that your Father also who is in heaven may forgive you your trespasses."[58]

---

[58] Mark 11:25

How could Jesus say such a thing? How could he link His forgiveness to our willingness to forgive? Does He not understand how others scar us or how their sin against us can mentally torment us?

My Personal Torment

This chapter is very personal, and I wrestled whether to include it. God answered my desperate teenage prayer. He gave me the solution that relieved me from tormenting thoughts.

I contemplated rehashing the story but decided against it. Even now, it stirs up unpleasant memories. One thing that helped me move on was when the story leaked to my football coach, and he saw to it the person was fired and left town.

Instead of telling you that story, I will share a series of true stories, with a few of the names and details changed to protect the innocent.

My freedom eventually came after I prayed for help. The Lord impressed upon me my need to forgive my offender.

This chapter is a little different than other chapters, because in addition to telling the story of an answered prayer, I hope to address a couple of the finer points of the process of forgiveness that some Christians overlook. My experience helped me to see these.

One of these finer points to the process is the importance of restitution. The other misconception I hope to examine is that forgiveness requires forgetting. I hope to make the point by the end of this chapter that forgiveness is given, but trust is earned, and that forgiveness does not require reconciliation.

The Burden of Holding On to an Offense

To withhold forgiveness is to hold a grudge, a debt. There is bitterness and a burden associated with carrying around a debt. When we carry it on our books, the person and the debt owed to us goes with us. The indebted party may be free from us, but because we carry the debt everywhere we go, we are not free from them.

Let me offer a spiritual warning to the person intent on holding a grudge. When we hold a grudge, we open a portal to the demonic that gives demons access to harass us with their demonic thoughts.

You want to close the door to demonic activity? Forgive the debt. Stop carrying it on your books. Free yourself from the offender. Let the Lord repay and restore.[59] I know what I am talking about here. Though I was an innocent boy at the time and did nothing wrong, the demons did not care that they had no right to put painful thoughts in my head to torture me.[60]

Not until I prayed for the Lord's help with these demonic, torturing thoughts did He put on my heart to forgive the offender. I did forgive and relief came. I was then able to see this person with pity instead of disdain and to forgive them and release them. When I did, it closed the door to tormenting thoughts, and I was free from the debtor and from painful thoughts.

A Burden to Forgive

I carried the load of the sin done to me. I also carried the burden to forgive. This doesn't seem fair, and it is not fair. When we are sinned against, the wound often lingers and festers. Little did I know, the healing doesn't begin until we are able to forgive.

And the Lord taught us how to pray: Forgive us our trespasses as we forgive those who trespass against us.[61] When the wound is fresh, we might say, "Really Lord? Are you serious? Do you know the harm they caused?"

---

[59] Romans 12:19
[60] II Corinthians 2:10-11
[61] Matthew 6:12

We might ask, why such a difficult command to an innocent victim? Just maybe, God knows it is the first step toward healing the innocent victim.

Linda's Story

Once upon a time, there was a beautiful girl named Linda. In my youth, I had the tendency to be drawn into a story where there was a beautiful girl.

Linda was talented and funny, and we liked many of the same things. However, there was something about Linda that took me by surprise. A short time after we met, she surprised me with her language. It was not a slip of the tongue like you might say when you stub your toe. Linda had language that would make a sailor blush.

Over the next week or so, I discovered that she had other bad habits too. Then she told me about hating Christians. "They are all just a bunch of self-righteous, judgmental people (not her exact words); I can't stand them," she said. She knew I was a Christian, and she was putting me on notice, but for some reason she liked me. We had a connection.

A few days later, she told me about her childhood and how her grandfather and grandmother were Christians. She told me that her grandfather constantly quoted scriptures.

Her grandparents were backwoods country folk who lived in rural Alabama. He was a mechanic. If he hadn't finished repairing a part, he would bring it into his bedroom to finish. She said grease and grime soiled the bed sheets.

The Confidence

She said, "The next thing I am going to tell you I have never told anyone. My grandfather used to molest me in that room on the greasy bed. And what is worse is that my grandmother knew it. She walked in on it and never said a word. And they were Christians, and he went around quoting scriptures. That bastard," she said, as her face contorted as if tortured by a demon. I could tell she had hated them both for a long time.

In what I can only describe as a divine insight, I said to her, "Do you think it is possible that your grandfather was fighting demons and the only way he knew how to fight was by quoting scripture?"

Her entire demeanor melted, and she said, "There is no doubt about it; he had demons." And with that admission, a spiritual transformation occurred in her, transforming from being angry to becoming compassionate. You know why she knew so quickly? She knew what it was like to fight demons. Those bad habits I discovered she had, those were pills that had become demons for her.

Linda went on to say that her grandfather's father left them when he was a small boy. His mother turned to prostitution to pay the bills. "He had seen a lot," she said. "He was abused on multiple occasions by both men and women coming in and out of his house." She began to see her grandfather in a totally new way. She had compassion for him.

That is the beginning of forgiveness. This is the beginning of freedom for the offended.

A Mistake Christians Make

Could you blame Linda if she didn't forgive her grandfather? Could you blame her for hurt turning to anger?

Even if she came to forgive her grandparents, would you expect it to be loving and normal? Forgiveness and trust are separate things. One is given; the other is earned over time. And reconciliation, that is another thing. It can only happen once the first two take place.

Please notice something else here. Christians can unwittingly grind salt into a person's wound. Because of Jesus' imperative that we must forgive, Christians tend to shift blame from the offender to the offended.

Some Christians advocate the offended party grant forgiveness automatically, including trust and reconciliation, if the offender asks for it. Here is the rub: We blame the offended party if they are not ready or willing to trust and reconcile. We insinuate they are derelict in their Christian duty to forgive and forget.

You may not have realized it, but twice the question was asked, "Can you blame her?" Why would it even enter our mind to blame Linda? Linda is innocent, a victim. However, in the Christian psyche, the victim gets blamed if they struggle to forgive, if they struggle to *just get over it*. This misunderstanding of God's directive to forgive is painful to an offended party struggling to heal.

Of course, it is for her own good if she will forgive. Hopefully, I added some perspective to help her forgive. It is unhelpful, and most likely destructive, to pressure her to trust or reconcile. Miracles do happen, but that must come to her on her own. My prayer is that she is moving toward a greater level of healing.

In a civilized society, it is imperative that we hold people accountable for their wrong actions. The grandfather and grandmother are the sinners in this instance and not this poor girl. Did their sin toward her exacerbate her own sin problem? It could be argued that it did.

Sadly, I know a battered woman whose Christian counselor advised her to go home with her husband because he said, "I'm sorry." It was not the first time he battered her. She went home with him and he beat her up again.

Forgiveness is given; trust is earned. To confuse those two makes for an unwise counselor.

The Story of John Croyle

I had the privilege of spending a day with John Croyle. Some of you might know him as the father of former Alabama and NFL quarterback, Brodie Croyle. John is a great man. He founded The Big Oak Ranch near Gadsden, Alabama, and helped raise 2,500 abused and abandoned kids.

"What motivates you?" I asked. He pointed to a newspaper clipping under glass on his desk. He said, "This is a story about a little girl whose father had badly beaten her. The judge released the little girl back into her father's custody because the man asked the judge to forgive him. He said to the judge, 'I am a changed man.' The little girl was dead within a week. That is why I opened The Big Oak Ranch for girls."

Forgiveness is given; trust is earned.

Story of Doug and Debbie

Doug and Debbie had a beautiful home. One day they came home to a house in shambles. A vandal broke into their home and took a baseball bat to the place. They broke cabinets and countertops, dishes and furniture. They went into the rooms that held their children's childhood trophies and smashed them all. Even their family pictures were dumped into the bathtub and set on fire.

It devastated Doug and Debbie when they returned home. They felt violated. They could replace the furniture, but the photos and the memories they stirred were lost forever.

Doug and Debbie put their life back together slowly. Within a week or so, you could hardly tell anyone had done such a senseless thing. They filed a police report, but it had been weeks with no suspect. Doug regularly came home to find Debbie crying. He noticed that she was jumpy, and she confided in him that she no longer felt safe there.

This feeling didn't go away and she began to talk about moving in to town. She wanted closer neighbors where she would feel safe.

The whole ordeal uprooted their family and disturbed their quality of life, as the increased distance from children and grandchildren made it difficult for them to drop by.

Two years later, a man knocks on Doug's door. The man appears to have a humble demeanor. He tells Doug that he has become a Christian and has a confession to make. He tells Doug he is the vandal. The man asks for forgiveness. He gives Doug a check for $5,000 for damages.

Doug looks him in the eye and says, "I forgive you, but $5,000 does not compensate me for all that I have lost. My wife's wounds are more than you could know. I appreciate your confession and your courage for coming forward, but I feel that it is appropriate that I report this to the authorities and let them prosecute you to the full extent of the law. I feel this is the best way for justice to be served."

Our hope as the offender is most always mercy, but is Doug justified in his response to a man asking for forgiveness? What about this idea of restitution?

The Purpose of Restitution

That takes us back to the words *penalty*, *fine*, *sentence*, and *restitution*. They are all a response to a wrong committed. Their purpose is to provide a consequence and a deterrent to wrong actions.

The idea of restitution comes from God. Moses established this principle as he was inspired to give laws and make judgments for his people. There are many examples of restitution, ranging from what to do if your ox falls in your neighbor's ditch, to what to do about damaged property.[62]

Under the Mosaic system, restitution helped right the wrong. The American legal system patterns itself after the Mosaic model. Our prisons are full of people paying restitution for crimes committed.

Luke tells us the story when Jesus met Zacchaeus.[63] Jesus accepts a dinner invitation from Zacchaeus, the wealthy tax collector. The Roman government contracted Jewish tax collectors to enforce the tax code. The Jews considered tax collectors traitors and cheats. They hated them for receiving a percentage as compensation for themselves.

After spending time with Jesus, Zacchaeus proclaims, "Behold, Lord, half of my goods I give to the poor. And if I have defrauded anyone of anything, I will restore it fourfold." And Jesus said to him, "Today, salvation has come to this house."

Zacchaeus repented, and his sincerity was evident in his immediate desire to make restitution. Here was a man who was penitent and contrite, and the proof of his conversion to Christ was his resolve to atone for past debts.

Making Amends

The same holds true for anyone who truly knows Christ today. Genuine repentance leads to a desire to redress wrongs committed. Not wrongs committed toward God, for those wrongs were redressed by the cross, but harm we caused others.

Jesus did not stop Zacchaeus and say, "Whoa. Just say you're sorry, ask forgiveness, and that is enough." No, Jesus understood the healing fostered through restitution for both victim and offender.

---

[62] Exodus 22:14
[63] Luke 19:1-10

Members of Alcoholics Anonymous understand this principle. It is so important to them that it takes up two of their 12 steps to recovery. They call it making amends for the wrongs you have committed to others. It goes like this: *Step Eight:* Made a list of all persons we have harmed and became willing to make amends to them all. *Step Nine:* Made direct amends to such people wherever possible, except when to do so would injure them or others.

Make It Right Before You Worship

I was fortunate to stand on the spot where Jesus offered his Sermon on the Mount, overlooking the beautiful Sea of Galilee. It is one of the most gorgeous places on the planet. It was there that Jesus said, "So if you are presenting your gift at the altar and remember there that your brother has something against you, leave your gift there before the altar and first go and be reconciled to your brother. Then come and offer your gift."[64]

First, go and reconcile with your brother. What does that mean? It could mean a number of things. It could be as simple as saying, "I was wrong. Will you forgive me?" It could require a sincere, "How can I make this right?" and allow the other person's input into restitution. Writing a check might remedy the situation. It could mean a confession that sends you to prison, as in the case of the vandal or the child-molesting grandfather.

The offender was to go immediately and make restitution before bringing his sacrifice to the Lord. This implies that making amends with one's neighbor is just as important as worshipping or making peace with God.

You may be wondering, did Jesus give us any words or examples regarding restitution?

---

[64] Matthew 5:23

The Cross Was Restitution

Sometimes we forget the cross is about restitution. The cross was Jesus paying restitution for the sinfulness of man to satisfy an offended God.

Remember Jesus' prayer to the Father in the Garden? Jesus certainly had a contrite heart. He tried to negotiate with God. We know He asked the Father to let this cup pass from Him.[65] He could have argued, "Father, I did nothing wrong. Isn't living a sinless life enough?" "No," was the Father's answer, and restitution was required. Thankfully, Jesus paid the price God required to satisfy His wrath and reconcile mankind to Himself.

The practice of AA is a wonderful one. It is full of wisdom and a recipe for reconciliation. Do you need to make a list of all the people you have harmed?

Do you need to make amends or restitution to someone you have wronged? Is your heart contrite? Or are you blame-shifting to the injured party for their inability to forgive and forget?

Jesus gives us the ideal when it comes to forgiving others. Hanging from nails with a crown of thorns pushed into his head, he said, "Forgive them, for they know not what they do."[66]

And He gives us the ideal for restitution: A willingness to do what it takes to reconcile, even pay an unfathomable price of a cross.

What Price Are You Willing to Pay to Help Restore a Relationship?

Leave your gift at the altar and go and reconcile with your brother or sister. What does it mean to leave your gift at the altar? In this

---

[65] Luke 22:42
[66] Luke 23:34

instance, the gift to God at the altar is a form of worship. What He is saying is, Get right with your brother or sister before you worship me. The burden of reconciliation is on the offender to do everything possible to make it right.

My Answered Prayer That Shaped My Life

The Lord answered my prayer for relief from tormenting thoughts by impressing upon me that I needed to forgive my offender. I did not realize that deliverance from painful thoughts would come after I forgave. The local employer took care of the restitution, which made forgiveness easier. In my situation, there was no need or desire for reconciliation. Fortunately, I learned how important forgiveness is and how it can set you free.

Epilogue

My friend Rex is on my advisor team and lives in Phoenix. We developed a friendship at business conventions we attended over a 15-year period. Rex had some questions for me on this chapter.

Rex: But if we don't forget, how do we forgive in the long run?

Clay: For me, it's about remembering my own need for forgiveness. There is much that I have needed to be forgiven for in my past, so I remember the fallen nature of all of us. Though I may not be able to forget an offense, I can choose to forgive. And if over time I see an indication that a person is repentant, which may include restitution, and they are making an honest effort to control their offensive behavior, I most likely will choose to reconcile and trust them again.[67] That is how I would want to be treated.

---

[67] Matthew 18:15-17

Rex: How do we respond when someone says, "What about Christ? He didn't forgive everyone."

Clay: But He did. That is both the beauty and the tragedy. Jesus has forgiven mankind of their sin,[68] yet many reject Him and His atonement for sin, and the curse of eternal death remains on them.[69]

Discussion, Reflection, and Actionable Suggestions:

1. Are you withholding forgiveness and carrying around a burden of debt? Are you ready to be free from it? If so, consider this prayer: Lord, I am tired of carrying this burden of debt. I ask you to repay the wrong done to me and help me to let it go and forgive. Assist me to see the person who did this with pity and help me to be free.
2. Forgiveness is given; trust is earned. Trust and reconciliation do not always go hand in hand with forgiveness. Discuss this concept.
3. Have you hurt someone so badly they will never trust you or desire reconciliation? If so, consider saying this prayer: Father, I take responsibility for my sinful actions, and I realize they may never trust me or desire a relationship. I pray for relief of this burden they carry and find a way to forgive -- not for me, but for themselves.
4. Is there someone you need to try to make amends to? Do you need to say you are sorry and ask forgiveness? Will writing a check make someone whole that you have damaged? Do you need to pay the penalty for a wrong you committed? If so, don't wait; do it now.

---

[68] I John 2:2

[69] John 3:36

5. Have you asked the Lord to come into your life to be your King? Have you confessed His name before men? Will you demonstrate your faith by public baptism? If you have not, consider this prayer: Dear Father, will you come into my life and be my King. I believe you are the true God and Jesus is your Son. Please give me direction as I seek to make my faith public.

9

The Unexpected Consequence of an Answered Prayer

Theology - the study of the existence and nature of the divine
and its relationship to and influence upon other beings.

YOU WOULDN'T THINK that a prayer ceremony where a person is healed would cause people to get upset and leave the church, would you? That is what happened. It happened because a healed woman caused a shift in theology.

Our theology, like an old pair of our brother's jeans, is a hand-me-down. It is not perfect. It is probably quite flawed. No person or church has perfect theology. Bad theology limits God.

Good theology strengthens our faith and relationship with the Lord and sheds light to those in darkness. Unfortunately, it is inevitable that an evolution in our theology will cause conflict, strained relationships, and bring on spiritual warfare.

The Prayer of Faith

The following is a story about prayer that took place when I was nineteen years old. It would shape my faith for years to come.

Janice is healed from cancer. She went to the doctor and came home with a report she had cancer. Her family felt demoralized. The church elders prayed for her, laid hands on her, and anointed her with oil. Janice gets her healing.

Our denomination didn't believe in modern-day miracles and some were afraid of the implications this healing would bring to the status quo.

Janice was our minister's wife. They were a young couple with small children. They were desperate for God to help them. When the minister pleaded in desperation, the elders of the small country church agreed to perform a New Testament-style prayer ceremony, complete with anointing oil and the laying on of hands.[70]

Our Small Rural Church

My dad was an elder at this little church. He was the best man I have ever known. He was not perfect.

My dad had a gift for leadership. People followed him. Get a dozen men doing almost anything, and within an hour, they would be looking to him for direction.

When I was ten, he and my mother took on the little rural church as their mission field. The church had about twelve members. My dad began preaching and teaching, and within two years, the church grew to 120 members. It was an exciting time in the life of this remote little community.

After a couple of years at the rural church, my dad began to groom Eddie, a local man in his mid-twenties, as our minister. He was an energetic, outgoing, and likeable young man. He was bright, and given an opportunity, could have been almost anything he wanted.

My dad and a few of his protégés would travel to Christian conferences where the men could learn from national thought leaders

---

[70] James 5:14

about our Christian tradition. Each week, Eddie became more dynamic and polished as a speaker. He obviously had a future as a Christian minister.

The Prayer Ceremony

Janice came home with her bad report during Eddie's third year as our minister. The whole church grieved for their situation.

It would be the first time in anyone's memory that our church, or any church in our denomination, had performed a prayer ceremony like this one. They gathered and anointed Janice with oil. They laid hands on her and asked the Lord to heal her of cancer.

The next week, she went in to begin her treatment. The physician group was flabbergasted when they retested Janice prior to treatment. Their new finding saw no signs of cancer. They called it miraculous. Our church went nuts, praising Jesus, and our faith in His desire to heal was high as a kite.

A Shift in Theology

Our theology shifted. This dramatic event shifted us from a church that believed in the cessation of miracles and spiritual gifts to a charismatic church.[71] At least this was the criticism we received by our sister churches. The reports came to my dad that our teachings and practices were heretical.

My dad was very sensitive to this criticism. He enjoyed the accolades he received from area churches who heard of the church's growth and his good work in this remote community. He didn't like criticism.

---

[71] Charismatic churches believe the gifts of the Holy Spirit continue today.

One criticism we heard was that our church had become Pentecostal.[72] That name conjured up negative stereotypes meant to sting. Being linked to Pentecostals embarrassed him.

Though our little church was growing rapidly in faith and numbers, my dad called a church meeting. In his statement, he said, "We will follow and teach the traditional doctrines of our church." As the chief leader among the church, he essentially shut down those who wanted to explore what it meant to operate in the spiritual gifts.

His decision turned out as the wrong decision for many in the little church, and over a period of a few weeks, half the church, many of which were new members, left to go somewhere else or stopped going to church altogether. Included in those who left was the minister and his wife Janice.

I asked my dad about the position he took and asked him for his rationale. He quoted one of the early founders from our movement regarding his stance on church unity. My dad's message was clear to me: He chose the status quo that would keep our church in good standing with our sister churches rather than go with uncertain change. Through my conversations with him over the years, I know he was ambivalent about his decision, but as leaders often do, they must live with their decisions whether right or wrong.

A few years later, I would tell him I was attending a church that actively pursued the gifts of the Spirit. I explained I needed to discover this for myself. He warned me that some in our church would persecute me. Fortunately, that never happened. Ultimately, I believe he was proud that I wasn't afraid of criticism.

---

[72] Pentecostal churches are a brand of charismatic church who are very distinctive in dress, and the more extreme factions handle snakes to prove their faith.

My Shift in Theology

I now have the vantage point of someone who has held both viewpoints. I have settled on the side of believing in the miraculous. My rationale for believing came from both what the Bible says as well as personal experience. My own experience tells me that God still heals and performs miracles for His beloved children. Many of the chapters in this book attest to this.

What does the Bible say? I have found the Bible is full of mystery and miracles, from Genesis to Revelation, from the miracle of Creation to His return in the clouds, and everywhere in between. I cannot find anywhere in the Bible where God says He will behave differently in the present time, though some have reasoned the Bible teaches this.

Many people think that the highest concentration of miracles in history happened during Jesus' life on earth. I think this is a faulty perception. The perception comes from the quality and quantity of recorded miracles surrounding a single person, Jesus. He was a miracle-producing phenomenon.

Today, Jesus is still a miracle-producing phenomenon, except that He is no longer limited to a single human being. His reach is now much greater, though diffused.

He is touching people in miraculous ways and in what could be said is an anonymous way. People call out to him in faith; He delivers, but without a single bodily person to receive the credit, and without indisputable evidence it was Him. Therefore, most miracles go undocumented because some fear others will think they are losing their marbles if they credit a miracle to Jesus. Yet, there are no doubt millions worldwide living today who claim a miracle from the hand of Jesus.

The Power of Faith

In many of the biblical accounts where people came to request healing, there is a common thread. Those healed had a high level of faith that Jesus had both the ability and willingness to heal. They believed something about him that caused them to have faith that He possessed this miraculous ability. And on seven occasions where Jesus healed, he proclaimed that it was their faith that healed them.[73][74][75][76][77][78]

The idea that it was their own faith that healed them has some controversial implications. Instead of the healing being a one-sided affair, Jesus gives credit to the power of faith. He acknowledges this power in faith and forces us to take notice of it. What is this mysterious power called *faith*. How do we measure it? How do we get more of it or strengthen it? Does God always respond to it? The answers remain unclear.

The Roman Centurion is a great example of Jesus responding to faith.[79] He comes to Jesus because of his paralyzed and suffering servant. The centurion is supremely confident in Jesus' ability. He too has faith in Jesus goodness and willingness. Jesus volunteers to go see the man's servant, but the centurion tells Jesus that is unnecessary and says, "All you need to do is say the word and he will be healed." This man had a remarkable understanding of who Jesus was. Jesus is surprised, and says, "I have not seen such great faith in all of Israel. As you have believed, so it will be done for you."

---

[73] Matthew 9:22
[74] Luke 17:19
[75] Luke 18:42
[76] Matthew 15:28
[77] Mark 5:34
[78] Mark 10:52
[79] Matthew 8:13

On the other hand, a deficiency of faith thwarts the miraculous. Matthew and Mark tell us about how the people from Jesus' hometown lacked faith in Him.[80] Their lack of faith somehow impeded the power of Jesus. Matthew simply writes that Jesus was unable to do many miracles in his hometown because of their lack of faith.

The Debate Continues

Today, the same two camps exist that have existed for all of history: The camp that believes in miracles and gifts of the Spirit, and the camp that does not.

Here is the irony: For the person who believes miracles have ceased, they have. And for the person with faith in Jesus' ability and willingness to do miracles, He still does.

For those of you reading who were taught miracles ceased with the death of the apostles, I have something for you to consider. Consider the people who were eyewitnesses to the miracles of Jesus and still did not believe. They were mostly religious Jews. The reason they didn't believe was because their high priest told them Jesus was not and could not be the Messiah.

This was a time they should have thought for themselves, instead of relying on the religious authority. This alone should at least cause one to remain open and seek more understanding.

Another Unfortunate Irony

In Luke 18, Jesus asked a haunting question. He asked, "Will I find faith on the earth when I return?" That signals, to me, that genuine faith in Jesus will be a rare quality by the time of His second coming.

---

[80] Matthew 13:8

There is no way to measure the level of a person's faith. It is invisible to the naked eye, and who can know how many pounds per square inch a person's faith can move. Why does it seem we may have enough faith for this and not for that?

Did this person have the measure of faith needed to accomplish the impossible, or was it something else? Did that person simply not have faith that moved a mountain or receive a cure? It is beyond knowing, and most Christians have experienced heartbreaking situations where prayers did not materialize. Some understand acutely how Jesus will one day need to wipe away their tears.

Keeping Peace with the Lord

It is supremely important to me to remain at peace with the Lord. More important than God answering my prayer for healing is my relationship with the Lord. I trust His character, His wisdom, and His goodness. Therefore, I must maintain a certain posture when approaching Him with my requests, and especially for healing. I must remember that He cares about people more than I do. He cares about me more than I do.

I must recognize my limited view and that He sees the big picture and like a chess master, He makes moves I could never understand to counteract the enemy and to set things up for ultimate victory. God is not a genie in a bottle. We cannot manipulate Him or approach Him with demands.

No one cheats death unless the Lord comes back first. Even Lazarus eventually died. So, all healing here on earth is temporary. That doesn't mean that God doesn't want to heal us from the sickness or disease that is here to cut our lives short or make us ineffective to do the work God has for us.

I acknowledge God can use sickness, and even death, to bless us and others. Sickness has a way of getting people to take stock of what they have built their life on. For some, this is their path to real faith in the Lord, because through sickness or death of a loved one, they see the error of their own way.

My prayer for healing would look something like this: Lord, I trust in you and in your goodness. I believe in your ability and willingness to heal us, but I know my faith is weak. Please strengthen my faith. I pray that you will heal in this situation, and that your will is done on earth as it is in heaven, and I will accept the outcome. I trust that whatever the outcome, you will work everything together for the good of all of us who love you.

Keeping the End in Mind

Jesus never scolded someone for having faith in Him in any circumstance, no matter how impossible the situation. He did, however, scold those with little or no faith.[81]

I live my life with a view that a day of accounting is coming. What that means to me is that there will be a day when Jesus will review my life and evaluate how well I lived it. Then he will reward accordingly.[82] If you have ever been to an award ceremony, then you know it is always better to be one who is receiving an award! I simply want as good a reward as I can get. Part of my strategy is that having faith and believing is a way of adding value to my future reward.[83]

The way I live my life can influence what the Lord says when I stand before Him one day. I had rather err on the side of believing in

---

[81] Matthew 8:26
[82] II Corinthians 5:10
[83] Hebrews 11:6

Him, His power, and His willingness to act on our behalf, than on the side of unbelief. The first position is certainly more defensible.

Three Winks

Immediately after I finished this chapter, a coincidence happened that I interpreted as a possible wink from God. By the end of the day, I received two more, and I was certain of it. Read about those three winks in the next chapter.

Epilogue One

You will get to know Chandler in this book because, as I mentioned, he has had a big impact on my life. We met through a mentor program when he was nine. He is now twenty-five and active in ministry, especially to foreign missions to Malawi, Africa.

Chandler: In my trips to Africa, I see much more belief in the spiritual realm among the African people. I held a baby there this past year that the people believe was born to a woman who was raised from the dead. The tribal leader in the village is a Christian, and he is the one who told us the story. I grew up not believing in modern-day miracles, but I do now.

Clay: Yes, there are many miraculous stories coming out of Africa. America may be more like the hometown of Jesus. The apostles said the faith of the people in Nazareth was so weak that Jesus was not able to do many miracles there.

Epilogue Two

Jeanette is my sister and a member of my advisor team. She calls to tell me the following:

Jeanette: Your last paragraph under the subheading *Keeping the End in Mind* is very weak.

The way I live my life can influence what the Lord says when I stand before Him one day. I had rather err on the side of believing in Him, His power, and His willingness to act on our behalf, than on the side of unbelief. The first position is certainly more defensible.

You are not very bold here, and it sounds like you have weak faith. You are saying you believe, but in reality, you are saying you believe just so you will have a defensible position before the Lord.

Clay: I suppose there is some truth in that. There have been times I felt like one of the disciples to whom a man brought his son who was possessed by an evil and demonic spirit.[84] The disciples were helpless to drive out the spirit that kept the boy in bondage. Jesus handled it, but not before scolding them for their unbelief.

Later, He told the disciples when they asked Him why they couldn't drive it out, "That kind can come out only by prayer."

So how confident am I when I come into life and death situations? Let's just say, not as confident as I would like to be. Like the boy's father in this story when the Lord said, "Anything is possible to those who believe." The boy's father replied, "Lord, I do believe; help me overcome my unbelief."

Discussion, Reflection, and Actionable Suggestions:

1. Has your theology grown as you have matured? In what ways? Has it had any big shifts or just minor tweaks?
2. Has a shift in theology caused waves with other people in your life?
3. Do you need a miracle in your life? Are you willing to trust the Lord enough to ask Him to move on your behalf in miraculous ways? Pray this prayer: Lord, I need a miracle, and you are the only one I know to turn to. I know there is power in faith, and I

---

[84] Mark 9:14-29

pray that you will give me faith to believe and strengthen my faith. You know my situation and what I need. I trust you to work it out. I will accept your answers. In Jesus' Name.

10

Three Winks

I RECEIVED THREE WINKS from God, bam-bam-bam, in one day, as I finished writing the previous chapter early on a Sunday morning.

What is a *wink*, you ask? Squire Rushnell wrote a book called, *When God Winks at You*. The book is about the little coincidences that you suspect are more than mere coincidence. You suspect it is God winking at you. Others call these *confirmations*, when it seems that the Lord is sending a message that you are on the right track and to keep going. Some say that one confirmation is good, two is better, and three over a short period is a sure sign the Lord is confirming you are on the right track.

I write in further detail about the significance of the number 3 in Chapter 21, but suffice it to say, the number 3 is the signature of God.[85]

Three Confirmations in One Day from Three Different People

It happened, like I said, as I was putting the finishing touches on the previous chapter. To refresh your memory, it was about a prayer for our minister's wife who was diagnosed with cancer. We prayed, and the

---

[85] The Number 3 - https://wp.me/p43B0F-Un

next report could not find any trace of cancer. Upon finishing the chapter, I received a text from my friend Rob Likens. Rob is a Southern Baptist. During his devotional time, he read a chapter in Mark Batterson's book *Grave Robber*. He thought to text the reading to me and three others for our input. This was not routine for Rob to send me something during his devotional. I can't remember the last time he did.

Wink One…

Rob's screenshot revealed the following:

"If you follow Jesus long enough and far enough, you will eventually trespass into the impossible. You'll turn water into wine, feed five thousand with two fish, and walk on water. I am not suggesting that you walk off the nearest dock and see how many steps you can take. God will probably manifest His power very differently for you than He did for the original disciples. But if you believe what Jesus said, then you will do what Jesus did. The miracles that you experience should be even greater than the miracles that Jesus performed, in terms of both quality and quantity."[86]

Wink Two…

A few minutes after Rob's group text, I received a text from Larry Marshall concerning the reading Rob sent. It contained these words:

"Wow! What a question this early on Sunday. Jesus proclaimed we could do greater things than He did, so I believe that. I saw my mother instantly healed while in a coma.[87] The doctors and our family believed she would die, but a young pastor walked into ICU and prayed for her healing, and in 24 hours she was in a regular room and ready to go home. I have personally addressed demons who were harassing or

---

[86] John 14:12
[87] John 14:12

controlling people. At Jesus' Name, they had to tell me their name, and I rebuked them and they left."[88]

I have read thousands of testimonies of healing, deliverance, and situational miracles that I believe are true. Jesus left us with POWER in the person of the Holy Spirit. Paul told us our weapons are not carnal but mighty for pulling down the strongholds of the enemy.[89] Jesus stated He came to set the captives free.[90] The miracles He performed did just that. I believe we can and do see miracles that we ask for, if it follows along that purpose to set "captives free." Also, we don't always see the end result of miracles, as the effects can stretch into future generations.

Wink Three...

Our fellowship group met on the same night, and Keith Davis, a new member, gave his story of how he came to faith. He then shared an additional story about the daughter of a co-worker. Diagnosed with sudden onset bacterial meningitis, she was miraculously healed. "They gave her only hours when the prayer warriors rallied," he said. "By the next morning, the daughter did not die, but instead, was sitting up in bed, calling for food because she was starving. She made a complete recovery."

It was surprising to get three coincidental winks from God on the very day I finished the chapter on the Lord's miraculous nature. As unusual as this was, what happened next (I share in the next chapter) I would clearly define as *bizarre*.

---

[88] John 14:13
[89] II Corinthians 10:4
[90] Luke 4:18

Epilogue

Larry just so happens to be a part of my advisor team. He made the following comment about the previous chapter:

Larry: We have similar backgrounds. When my mother was healed on her deathbed, the leaders of their church told my dad to not be so exuberant because the person who prayed was not a member of their church, as if that mattered to us.

The only thing I might suggest to improve this discussion is expanding why people don't believe in praying for miracles or in spiritual gifts. You might explain why certain churches are fearful of miracles.

Clay: I would just suggest that people study what is known as the "Cessationist" viewpoint and study the "Continuationist" viewpoint. A few years ago, I was privileged to hear Jack Deere, author of *Surprised by the Holy Spirit,* and a former Cessationist turned Continuationist. He said if you lock a new believer in a room with only a Bible for a year, he would not come out a Cessationist. I think even a Cessationist would have to agree with that.

To add a little historical perspective to this discussion, the Cessationist "doctrine" was solidified by the Protestant reformers. You must remember that the reformers were in a battle to refute the authority of the papacy and his infallibility. To strengthen this position, they contended that continuation of the apostles, prophets, miracles, and spiritual gifts ended with the twelve apostles. The Bible itself never makes this claim.

To the contrary, Peter, the apostle, quotes a 900-year-old prophecy from Joel regarding what he called the last days...the days leading up to Jesus return. In those days, Peter says, God will do great things for people. He will give some knowledge of future events, some visions and others dreams, and what he called an outpouring of the Spirit, when all that call on the Name of Jesus will be saved.[91] The Father is so welcoming and makes it so easy for people to be reconciled with Him, if they will.

Discussion, Reflection, and Actionable Suggestions:

1. Have you ever experienced circumstances that seemed that God may be winking at you?
2. It is common to hear people talk about things happening in threes. Have you ever noticed this and wondered if there was significance to it?
3. Are you open to experiencing the impossible?

---

[91] Acts 2:17-21

11

Self-Substantiation
What in the World Is That?

I WASN'T PREPARED FOR the resistance when I shared the stories of Chapters 9 and 10 with my small fellowship group. It became obvious that a couple in the group felt very uncomfortable with the association of healing with faith.

One said, "I don't believe that a person is not healed because of a lack of faith. I have seen lots of people who had faith and were not healed. I remember when Pastor Bill died with ALS. The whole community was standing in faith for his healing, yet he was not healed. For some, it is their time to go and he was ultimately healed."

I agree, for some it is their time to go, and I have faith that all Christians go into the next life healed. However, I am still unwilling to say there is no connection between faith and healing. There are too many biblical examples to the contrary.

Pastor Bill's illness was a very high-profile case in our area. He was a local Southern Baptist pastor who received a diagnosis of ALS. It shocked the whole community, and prayers for faith and healing were going out everywhere. Bill's wife was leading the charge to believe for Bill's healing.

There were even bumper stickers that said, "Pray for Bill." I was doing a morning television show during that time, and we had Bill and Laura on television talking about the illness and how they were praying for healing. Laura was the boldest in their position for what they were asking from God. To me, Bill seemed to be managing expectations and tempering the emotional fallout if he wasn't healed. As usual, Bill was thinking of others.

Unfortunately, Bill did not receive healing from ALS, though many would acknowledge that he did receive ultimate healing as he moved to his new life with the Lord.

It has been over fifteen years since Bill's death. Laura has since remarried and moved to another state, though we touch base occasionally through Facebook.

Our Facebook Conversation

Knowing Laura's faith and her penchant for teaching, I decided to ask her what she had learned from this experience about faith, prayer, and healing. I contacted her the only way I knew how -- through Facebook. The following is our conversation and what would become the answer to another prayer:

Clay: Hi Laura, Looks like you are doing good these days. I see you as much on FB as I do the people who live right here. Would you mind if I ask you a personal question?

Apr. 10th, 10:20 a.m.

Laura: No...I don't mind.

Clay: I am writing another book. The working title is *Answered Prayers that Shaped My Faith*. I am working on a chapter about a woman healed of cancer. The healing came after a prayer ceremony with anointing oil and laying on hands. I was wondering what lessons you learned about prayer, faith, and healing from what you and Bill went through....not that I want to write about it...but that was such a high-profile ordeal and I would like to learn what you learned.

Laura: As you know, the prayer 'effort' for Bill's healing was intense, and we did not get the outcome we wanted. What I learned about prayer (for healing) is that there are always hidden issues we cannot see. We tend to think of 'prayer' as us, down here, begging God, up there, to DO something.

What I know now is that prayer is a judicial exercise before a court, and if there are charges against the person that are not dealt with, justice must prevail, no matter how much you cry and plead and quote scripture (a judge is not moved by tears, only by evidence). Sometimes those charges are coming from generational sin in one's bloodline ('the sins of the fathers visited upon the children to the 3rd and 4th generation'...this is in the OT twice).

These are 'curses' and they are real. Satan's official name (in Hebrew, I think) is 'Ha-sa-TAN,' which literally means 'prosecuting attorney'...this is his JOB. If he has legal right to oppress or inflict, [and this] is not removed or nullified, the answer you seek will not manifest. An EXCELLENT teaching about this is found on YouTube (Robert Henderson, 'Navigating the Courts of Heaven'). Sickness and disease are all part of the 'curse' of sin.

Jesus 'became a curse' for us, so LEGALLY we are immune to the curse of sin, but what Jesus accomplished on the Cross is like a LEGAL DECREE...but it must be enforced.

Just because a court orders something doesn't mean the other side just backs away; it must be applied and enforced. I'm not saying if I had understood all this we would have had a different outcome with Bill...we may have, but also, every man has a set number of days to live on the earth. SO... regarding what I learned, I learned to ALWAYS trust in the goodness of God, even when it 'feels' like He's 'slaying' you (this always pleases Him) ...and I also learned there is way more to seeing supernatural activity on the earth than simply quoting some scriptures and wanting it with all your heart.

Clay: Wow...what a thoughtful response. After I asked the question, I regretted it. 'You are aggravating deep wounds,' I thought. Then I heard another voice that said, 'I trust Laura and her relationship with the Lord and His goodness toward her.' Thanks for sharing that. I have noticed that there is a raw sensitivity among people today over the subject of faith and healing. People are chafed already when someone broaches the subject. Thank you for your insights.

Laura: But we DID see answered prayer and great grace...if you can have a 'good case' of that awful disease he did; able to move his legs and arms and walk a little (with help) till the end. Still lots of misery, but never total paralysis.

The Courts of Heaven

Clay: Hi Laura, I watched a two-hour message from Robert Henderson. It has a ring of truth. Have you learned to pray like this? Do you have any experience with quicker breakthroughs? It does magnify the power of the blood as a practical matter. I am still trying to digest. Thanks for sharing.

Laura: Yes, I always approach any needs now from a judicial perspective and we have seen some breakthroughs that have been rather sudden, but it still requires perseverance.

I'm also learning to pray from God's purposes rather than from my need, which is very important.

There is another powerful and simple message on this on YouTube. It is by a woman who had a pretty dramatic revelation from the Lord when praying for her daughter. I believe the title is 'From the Courtroom of Heaven to the Throne of Mercy and Grace.' (The author of this video is Anzel Spiller.)

She had always been a pretty strong intercessor, but God spoke to her very vividly in a dream that she needed to shift to a courtroom view for her wayward daughter, and she saw dramatic results within 7 days.

Clay: I just talked to the Lord about what Satan was accusing me of.....18 things came to mind easily. I have some repenting and praying to do.

Laura: Good news: the Judge is your daddy and He's looking for any reason to acquit you.

Clay: That is good news.

Laura: Good news, indeed!!

The Following Day - Self-Substantiation

Clay: Ok...I may have gotten you into something here.... or you got me into something. Just need your thoughts. Remember me telling you there were 18 things that came to mind where Satan could accuse me? Afterward, I thought, 'Some of these things I have dealt with and taken to the Lord years ago.'

Then last night I prayed that the Lord would give me a dream about the Courtroom of Heaven. I woke up this morning a little disappointed I had not dreamed. However, it hit me that a phrase kept repeating itself over and over in my head. It was an unfamiliar phrase. The phrase was *self-substantiation*.

I was unfamiliar with the phrase, so I googled it and pulled up some very weird philosophical stuff about the theory of the existence of everything. Then I looked up the word *substantiation*. The simple definition is *to prove the truth of something*. Additional definitions are: 2. *To give evidence or testimony to the truth or factualness*. 3. *To gain full recognition or acceptance of*. 4. *To show the existence or truth of by evidence*. There is obviously some legal jargon here. Anything jump out at you?

Laura: Got to leave for work, but I had to take a minute to google *self-substantiation* myself. THIS is the first thing that came up: *the act of a blue pill becoming aware of and/or escaping from the Matrix, without any external help or means.*

I haven't looked at the source, but THIS makes perfect sense to me. Bob and I feel as if that's exactly what we've been doing the last 3 years...escaping from the Matrix of THIS reality to experience the TRUE heavenly realities where our citizenship already lies. We "sit" with Christ there...already! No time for more, but I will look into this further.

Laura, later that day: Another thing it could refer to, in the legal sense (to prove the truth of something), is where the scripture says, "Agree with your adversary QUICKLY" ...so, even though you've 'repented' of these things, just stand there by faith in court and AGREE with every accusation. You are SELF-SUBSTANTIATING what the prosecuting attorney is saying about you.

THEN you appeal to the Blood for mercy and RECEIVE the verdict of the court...NOT GUILTY. Sometimes those things will come up again (new accusations) when we give into them again (things like pride, independence from God...these are things I repeatedly fall back into). So, you just do that same thing again...AGREE with the accusation (because it's true) and accept an innocent verdict based upon the Blood.

THEN, you are ready to do business in court about your issue. We always need to deal with personal accusations first so we will be clothed with the righteousness of Christ as we plead our case.

Clay: Yes, *self-substantiation* is simply another way of saying *confession*. I have substantiated to the Lord the claims or evidence made against me by my accuser. The Lord knew this was the key to defeating Satan in court. Simply confess your sins and He is faithful to forgive. This is amazing, for I would have never conjured the word *self-*

substantiation in a million years. And the Lord knew I might have ignored the word *confession* if that had been the word that kept repeating itself. Self-substantiation was such a foreign expression to me that I couldn't ignore it.

Laura: Fasten your seat belt...the Lord is revealing amazing things to our generation...truths that have been hidden.

Discussion, Reflection, and Actionable Suggestions:

1. For some, it is their time to go and they are ultimately healed.
2. Do you need to agree with the accuser who accuses you of sin before the throne of God? Are you willing to ask the Lord to judge you with mercy and grace instead of justice because the Lord has taken the penalty of your sin on the cross?
3. The Lord got the author's attention in a very unusual way. Can you think of a time when unusual circumstances made you wonder if God was trying to tell you something?
4. Would you like for the Lord to communicate with you in new ways? Consider this prayer: Lord, help me to be attuned to hearing you in any way you choose to communicate. Give me ears to hear what you have to say. In Jesus' Name.

12

Sometimes We Are Not Ready for the Answer

Trust in the Lord with all your heart, and do not lean on your own understanding. In all your ways acknowledge him, and he will make straight your paths.

-- Proverbs 3:5-6

"WHAT DO YOU WANT to be when you grow up?" I asked nine-year-old Chandler.

"I am going to be a doctor and a rock star."

"Both of those take a lot of time, don't you think?"

"I am going to be a doctor in the daytime and a rock star at night."

I didn't have the heart to break it to him that the odds of his dream coming true is one in a billion, so I let him keep his fantasy.

When we are young, some of our prayers must sound just as farcical to the Lord. Have you ever prayed for something and you didn't get it? Or at least it didn't look like what you asked for when you received it?

Role Models

Who knows why we want the things we want for ourselves? Often, at a young age, we meet someone and can identify with them. These role models are important to our future selves, because we desire to be like them. We often do what we see them doing. Without fully understanding how God works, it seems obvious He uses our affinity for role models to start us down a path.

This affinity for our role models can motivate us to pray to be like them. Little do we comprehend the time and painful difficulties a prayer like that may entail. Sometimes we pray for things and it is obvious we are not ready to receive an answer. Though the Lord may plant the seed, it takes time for Him to prepare us to receive our answer. During this lengthy process, the seed (our vision for ourselves) may appear dead and buried before it germinates, begins to root itself, and show signs of life.

Out of all the possible career paths, by the eleventh grade, I wanted to be an insurance agent for State Farm Insurance. It makes me laugh now, not because it was not a good and honorable pursuit, but because there were so many more viable options in hindsight. It is ironic that we must make our most important decisions with very little experience to base them on.

If you knew my family history, you might think this would be a natural choice for me, because my dad was a successful insurance agency owner. But in addition to my father's influence, State Farm had a policy of hiring high-profile athletes from Alabama and Auburn. By my junior year, I heard Pat Sullivan, the former Heisman Trophy winner from Auburn, was a State Farm agent. So I prayed and determined that is what I would do and be. On a scrap of paper, the prayer was recorded and tucked away in my billfold as a reminder.

Have You Ever Prayed For Something and the Journey to Receiving It Seemed Long and Hard?

In college, the goal of working for State Farm remained my focus. My college didn't have a degree in insurance, so a double major in finance and marketing made logical sense. Dr. Gerald Crawford, my marketing professor, encouraged me when he said, "Clay, you are my brightest marketing student. I will do everything in my power to help you get the job you want." I seized the offer by telling him my desire to work for State Farm. He called Pete Milligan, the State Farm statewide agent recruiter in Birmingham, and convinced him he should interview me.

Out of respect for Dr. Crawford, Pete Milligan of State Farm agreed to see me, but the interview didn't turn out as I had hoped. Mr. Milligan explained to me that it was company policy not to hire agents out of college. Their policy was to hire married men (before the days of gender equality) in their late twenties and early thirties, with an existing track record for success in business. I tried every angle and pulled every string to influence him to change the requirements, but he would not relent.

Rejected and Dejected

Dejected, I turned to my old college roommate, Jimmy Holland. He worked with Metropolitan Life, and his dad, Jimmy, Sr., led the company nationally in sales. Jimmy's uncle, Mike Holland, hired local agents.

To my surprise, Mr. Holland was not that interested in me either. He reluctantly allowed me to take the psychological profile tests they give to prospective agents. "According to the profile tests, Clay, you are not cut out for the insurance business or for sales," Mr. Holland informed me.

Not ready to give up, I persisted to ask him for a chance. Finally, he said, "Okay, come in here on Monday with six appointments. If you can't get six, then there is no reason wasting our time." The pressure was on.

Baptism by Fire

It occurred to me the university had a list they would make available of all the parents of my fellow students who shared my church affiliation. Of course, all these parents are good and kind people who will want to help me and give me an appointment to sell them insurance, right? You could say I was a touch naïve.

All day, I dialed the phone, calling one person after the other. I called 109 people before six people agreed to see me for an appointment. I know what you sales executives are thinking. You are thinking, "Hey, that's pretty good. That is the normal ratio of appointments to cold calls."

What you don't know is that I did not have that perspective. It was 103 confirmations that I was a failure at this profession. I knew nothing about call ratios. I cried myself to sleep that night like a boy who had lost his way in the woods. Now, in the career I thought I always wanted and prayed for, I had two validations that I was no good at it. The tests said I couldn't do it, and now the people I contacted do not want to talk to me.

I was in a spiritual battle and didn't even know it. The Bible says that for lack of vision, my people perish.[92] Another word for *vision* is *perspective*. What I desperately needed in this critical moment was proper perspective from a wise advisor. The devil's attack can derail you when you are young and naïve and without a good advisor.[93]

Another Failure

The next day I took the supplies back to Metropolitan Life. "You were right," I said to Mike Holland, putting the supplies on his desk. "I

---

[92] Hosea 4:6
[93] Proverbs 11:14

am not cut out for this business." Until then, my vocabulary didn't include the word *failure*. Round one belonged to the devil, and my prayer was dead.

Dejected, my confidence reeled from the setbacks. The economy didn't help either. It was 1980 and the economy was in serious recession at the end of Jimmy Carter's presidency.

My desire was to stay in the area. That's where my girlfriend lived. A job opened as an assistant manager in the men's department at a large retailer, and I took it. My ego was embarrassed to sell clothes in the mall. I did that before I had a diploma. Every day I felt like a failure. After all, I was Dr. Crawford's brightest marketing student. My girlfriend wasn't too impressed either. She started dating my best friend.

After a few months, I began studying for the real estate exam and passed it on the first try. It turned out to be another complete failure. My commission-only real estate job lasted six months with no sales, and my meager savings depleted. Out of money, it made sense to accept a job in my hometown and move back in with my parents. I was on a roll.

More of the Same

After a year of being back home with my parents, my brother brought me in to help rescue his struggling business in Houston, Texas. After eighteen months, we were bankrupt.

Just prior to bankruptcy, I bought a house in Houston (It would later be in foreclosure). To make ends meet, I took a job as a sign salesman, but quit after becoming seriously depressed and sleeping twelve-plus hours a day.

The next move was to Birmingham, Alabama, about the time of telephone deregulation and the breakup of AT&T. The spin-off telephone companies were hiring representatives to sell long distance telephone service. Again, within a few weeks, the depression sent me home to sleep it off.

A business plan I put together helped persuade my brother into quitting his job to open an insurance agency and a used car dealership in our small hometown. We struggled, and within a year, I abandoned him to take a promising job with a salary. My brother was forced to shut down the business a few months later. It was a tough time for him and his family, primarily because I chose self over honor.

My failures were adding up. In my wake, the carnage being left behind was not good. Had He heard my prayers? Was God leading me through all this failure?

Another Near Failure

The salaried position was as a health insurance sales executive with the Humana Corporation. We all worked hard for two years to establish Humana in the market. After we achieved this, Humana asked me to move to another market. Our success in the market helped me to gain a new belief and confidence I could be good at this.

Instead of moving to a new city with Humana, I decided to go back out on my own as an independent agency owner. New partnerships were formed, and we bought an office building to accommodate my optimistic plans for growth. Within only two years, we came to the brink of bankruptcy yet again. Due to a variety of reasons, we all went our separate ways and dissolved our partnership. Chapter 19 tells this story in greater detail and the result of another answered prayer.

A Turning Point

Things did eventually begin to turn (covered more fully in Chapter 19). I did not go bankrupt or lose the office building. New people and opportunities presented themselves, and we began to grow and prosper. For twenty years we grew, and our blessings exceeded even my expectations -- so much so that others began to notice.

Starting out, I hardly knew how to pray or what to pray for. All I knew was to pray and set my sights on what looked like a good thing to do with my life. It was a means to support a family. At times the way was very hard and I needed to grow in experience, work ethic, knowledge, and attitude. It always felt like I was in the Lord's management training course. Looking back, I wouldn't change a thing.

Epilogue One

After over twenty years in the insurance industry, the Alabama Association of Insurance and Financial Advisors asked me to give the keynote speech at their annual convention in Orange Beach, Alabama. In the speech, I included this story about my early desires to work for State Farm and the rollercoaster ride that led me back to the industry. It was my hope to help other agents by sharing my perspectives and the things that had been successful for me. At the end of the speech, the ballroom crowd gave me a standing ovation.

After the speech, a man approached me. He said, "My name is Tom Johnson with State Farm, and I hold the same statewide position that Pete Milligan did when you asked for the job. I want you to know that Pete Milligan made a big mistake by not hiring you."

It would have been difficult to wipe the big smile off my face as I left the resort that day. Upon reflection, it seemed this part of my life had been scripted. It was as if I had been a character in a feel-good story. This story was evidence to me that, despite the flawed person in the story, bringing pain upon himself and others, the Lord worked it out for good in the end. Getting to where our prayers are taking us can be painful at times. Sometimes the growth necessary to get there is both painful and exhilarating. The process humbled and changed me. It gave me another reason to believe I have a faithful Father in heaven looking after me.

Epilogue Two

It was around 7:45 this morning when I finished writing this chapter. It is my plan to share this story with my fellowship group tonight. After finishing the chapter, I opened Facebook to check messages.

Out of the blue, Mike Holland, the retired manager for Metropolitan Life, sent me a friend request. Mr. Holland and I haven't bumped into each other in ten years. It has been 37 years since my original interview with him. It is as if the Lord winked at me today and said, "Just letting you know you are on the right track. Glad you noticed it was Me."

Discussion, Reflection, and Actionable Suggestions:

1. Who were your early role models, and did they influence your early goals or prayers?
2. Was finding your way after your school years filled with failure and setback? Did you have a sense God was teaching you and preparing you for the future?
3. I often hear people say they didn't end up using their education like they expected to. What was your experience?
4. Was there a time when you could have really benefited from a wise mentor who could give you perspective on your situation? Are you mentoring a younger person in your life?
5. Are you young and just starting out? If so, say this prayer: Lord, I need your guidance, wisdom, and many other things that I don't even know how to ask for. Put people in my life to help guide me. Help me to be a quick learner. Give me wisdom.

Help me to trust you that you will work everything together for my good and that you are always with me. In Jesus' Name.

13

There is No Victory Without a Battle

"'Don't be afraid, Daniel,' he told me, 'because from the first day that you committed yourself to understand and to humble yourself before your God, your words were heard. I've come in answer to your prayers."

-- Daniel 10:12

AS MENTIONED IN THE PREVIOUS chapter, my dream job lay shattered by age twenty-three. Then came another quick failure in insurance and a humbling stint in retail. The real estate business offered me another speedy failure and a depleted savings account. My most promising move looked like moving back in with my parents.

My father's old rustic farmhouse became my refuge. In the corner of the bedroom was a rug and a chair I rescued from the garbage heap. On my knees, with elbows in the chair, I poured out my heart, asking for opportunities that met my expectations and the courage to take a step toward one. Day after day, during my lunch break from the manufacturing plant, I went to the rug and chair to pray.

My high school nemeses, once jealous of me, were now smiling. From the outside, I looked like a loser. My confidence was no doubt shaken, but on the inside there was something beginning to rise.

Romans 8:28

A linebacker from the Miami Dolphins helped shape my perspective years earlier. He was God's angel, showing up at age fourteen, with the answer to my prayer for wisdom.

My dad was the emcee of an athletic banquet featuring Mike Kolen as speaker. Dad asked him to sign an autograph for me. Underneath his name he wrote *Romans 8:28*.

This verse reads, "All things work together for good to those who love the Lord and are called according to His purposes." Romans 8:28 became my motto from that moment on. From then on, if I signed a school book annual or a friend's cast, under my name I wrote *Romans 8:28*. Mike Kolen's routine autograph unknowingly provided a seminal moment for me. It built in me an inner confidence that the Lord was on my side.

My perspective viewed everything as working together for my good. There could only be ultimate success with the Lord as my mentor. Failure was no longer failure, but a stepping stone to eventual success. The way the verse inspired me to perceive my circumstances was a powerful motivator, prodding me to move ahead.

At least after moving back in with my parents, I had a job. The job in manufacturing was an excellent learning experience and a natural progression in my development. Assistant sales manager in a furniture manufacturing plant was the next assignment the Lord used to train me.

It was extraordinary exposure for me to work with the manufacturing reps. The primary links to the customer, these seasoned pros were indispensable to our company. Meticulously, they trained me, not because it was their job, but because my performance was important to their customer and their compensation.

Though the job had excellent potential, it felt like a step backward in my growth as a man. It felt too safe back in my hometown, and I hated the stigma of living with my parents again.

With my self-confidence wounded, a spirit of fear welled up inside and threatened to immobilize me. The comfort and safety of the daily routine lulled me into a false sense of security. Feelings of fear gripped me when considering a move out into the bigger and more dangerous world. I was ambivalent watching other friends striking out on their adventures. The noose began to tighten, and an uncomfortable feeling wormed its way in.

I am persuaded the Lord uses discomfort as a tactic for gaining our attention. It helps to emotionally prepare us for the big jumps we need to make. To quote Bilbo Baggins: He prepares us "to go far over the misty mountains cold, to dungeons deep and caverns old."[94]

The Big Offer

My oldest brother Joel was quite an entrepreneur. He lived in Denver and worked as an engineering consultant to the oil and gas industry. In addition, he owned three oil field service businesses in Houston, Texas.

Joel knew about my dissatisfaction at work. He was always trying to coax his siblings onto a bigger stage. "Clay," he called me on the phone one day, "Will you help with my businesses in Houston. I don't trust the people leading my companies, and I fear they are running them in the ground. I need eyes and ears in Houston I can trust. The company will pay you twenty-five percent more than you are making."

"What would I do?" I asked. "You would be our vice president of sales, calling on engineers at major oil companies like Exxon and Shell." "Would I have to live in Houston?" the fear made me ask. "At first, but

---

[94] The Hobbit

New Orléans is in the center of your territory. You can live there once you are established." "Give me until Friday to think about it," I said.

On Friday I called Joel and accepted the job. My mom and dad knew about the offer, but we had not discussed it. My mom tried to be supportive, though her attention was focused on back pain, recently sidelining her from work. It seemed obvious my dad was not on board.

My father remained quiet as I packed to move. I felt what he was thinking. He was losing me the same way he had lost Joel. His youngest son, too, would move to Texas and be out of his life except for once a year or so. Being the youngest, born sixteen years after my oldest brother, my dad and mom were older by the time of my graduation. Forlorn at the thought of being that far away from them during their last days, I began to grieve on the inside.

By Saturday, my car was packed from top to bottom. My father busied himself silently in his shop. It felt like he was withholding his blessing. The magnitude of the decision to move that far away was bearing on my emotions. I thought about my parents and missing their last years. Finally, my emotions overflowed into tears to my mother, "I don't want to leave you. I don't want to miss your last days." So I unpacked my car and called my brother to break the news. My decision pleased my dad, though he never said so.

Was It Love or Fear That Kept Me From Leaving?

I wondered if it was love or fear. Fortunately, they gave me my job back at the furniture manufacturing plant, but I became more and more unsettled. There was a stirring on the inside. I turned again to prayer. Something needed to change.

An abandoned farmhouse sat on my father's farm. It had become my remodeling project. It would also be my prayer retreat. Those prayers, offered during my lunch break, laid the groundwork for me over the next two years. These two years would mature me and go a long way toward shaping my future faith.

Within six months, I found the courage to step out and take the position my brother offered. The move to Houston would mean a move to a place without any family or friends. Intellectually, it was reasonable to think I was helping my brother while making more money. Emotionally, it scared me to death to take this leap into a world inhabited by aliens.

By now, my father knew that it was best for me to go. In so many words, he finally gave his blessing. My mother, whose back pain had worsened, had one suggestion for me. She said, "This is my prayer for you, Clay. Find a church and make that church your family."

My mother's back pain turned out to be cancer and the diagnosis came shortly after my move to Houston. Two weeks after the diagnosis she died. Those extra six months with them were memorable and precious times -- and they were her last days.

Was it gratifying to my parents to learn the depth of love and appreciation I had for them? Did the Lord help orchestrate that? Was it God's love and mercy to give us the extra time while she was sick?

The answers to those questions seem obvious to me. God is a loving Father who cares, and He orchestrated events to answer my mother's prayers and our prayers for her. He was also answering my prayers for my future. One thing is certain to me: Something changed to open the door for me to leave. And the way was paved when I arrived in Houston.

It Is Not Always As It Seems

What looks like retreat after a defeat may be something else. When I don't know what else to do, I call on the Lord to fight our invisible foe. I trust Him to send out His angels to battle for me. I understand it can take time to see results.[95]

I have confidence and faith that Jesus has already won the ultimate battle.[96][97][98] Salvation and eternal life were secured for the one who has been born again into Christ.[99] However, we continue to fight a fight of faith.[100] This invisible battle could be raging all around us and bigger than we know.[101]

Our understanding is so limited with regard to what we face.[102] The best I know to do is to lean on the best people I can, follow their counsel, and seek the help of the mighty Helper to be my spiritual eyes, to deliver me from evil, and lead me away from temptation. Without this Helper, we could be ambushed from any direction. We all know people who were poorly equipped to handle life's issues who were cut to shreds.

It was Jesus' brother James who told believers to consider it pure joy when we face a trial.[103] He said the testing of our faith produces perseverance and leads to maturity and having the spiritual necessities. In essence, we win the battle of faith step by step and little by little as He goes with us and as our faith grows.

Epilogue

Over 30 years after graduation from high school, a classmate called me to say she wanted to talk about God. Her life was in a hard spot and

---

[95] Daniel 10:13
[96] I Corinthians 15:57
[97] Romans 8:37
[98] Hebrews 2:14
[99] II Corinthians 5:17
[100] I Timothy 6:12
[101] Ephesians 6:12
[102] I Corinthians 13:12
[103] James 1:2-4

she had made a significant number of poor decisions. Her latest poor decision left her desperate and in jeopardy of doing jail time. She told me I had signed her high school annual and put *Romans 8:28* under my name. She said she had known the Lord when she was younger but had been running from Him for years. She wanted to talk.

A few days later I paid her a visit, and it was obvious her circumstances had her attention and she was searching. There is little about the conversation I remember, but soon after that her path led her to make a remarkable turnaround in her life. We stay in touch and her faith has grown by leaps and bounds. Hopefully, I played a small part in her journey home, and inadvertently, so did Mike Kolen, by simply signing his name and directing me to the Lord. We all plant seeds not knowing the kind of ground it will find.

Discussion, Reflection, and Actionable Suggestions:

1. What fears are holding you back? Like the author did, would you consider dedicating time to spend with the Lord in prayer to pour out your fears and concerns?
2. Have you experienced what seemed like terrible circumstances, but turned out as a great blessing?
3. Like the author did, are you willing to make Romans 8:28 a motto for your life and see all circumstances as a tool God can use for good?
4. Are you willing to see failures as stepping stones to success?

14

Mama Prayed

"See, I am sending an angel ahead of you to guard you along the way and to bring you to the place I have prepared."

-- Exodus 23:20

"I PRAY YOU QUICKLY FIND a church and make those people your family," was my mother's sage prayer as I packed to leave home for Houston. The following events are beyond coincidence.

Sometimes it is the prayer of someone who loves us that shapes our faith. When you don't know how to pray, it is a great blessing to have someone who loves you and knows how to pray for you. When we are young and embark on an adventure without close support from friends and family, we need special help. We can feel anxious with doubts and fears, but through prayer, the Lord will put people in our path as guides to help us traverse the unfamiliar terrain.

The Fight of Faith

In previous chapters, I shared my early fight of faith. My prayers did not seem to create an easy path; instead, when I prayed, I felt opposed and surrounded by what felt like a spiritual battle. It is more likely that my prayers were impetuous and short-sighted. The struggle caused me to wonder, "Is the Lord hearing my prayers? Is God willing to answer? Will He allow me to be a miserable failure?" And the big question from Satan, "Is God a good Person, and does He really care?"

In hindsight, what we call failures are not failures at all. For a child of God, whose life is orchestrated by Him, the better term is *stepping stones*. These stepping stones are for learning how to pray and learning the will of the Lord for our lives. It is not unlike the baby who learns how to walk. We don't panic every time a child loses his balance and falls, even when he cracks his head on a table or chair, because we understand it is part of the learning process.

Yet, if we are not wise to the learning process, here is where we find a lot of disappointment in our life. What may seem like unanswered prayer may be for our learning, or even protection from God. Why else would the Spirit tell us to "give thanks in all circumstances, for this is God's will for you?"[104]

Here is where the devil attacks our faith in the Lord. This is when he whispers in our ear, "This is all there is. God does not care about you. He has failed you. Curse God and die and get it over with."[105] Instead, God knows you are only getting started.[106] Temporary hardship here is simply a part of the necessary testing of the faith it takes to move into the next realm.

Learning How to Pray

It is perfectly normal for beginners to pray like beginners. My requests for a motorcycle to my biological father started at age ten. He waited almost an eternity to grant my request. He bought a mini-bike

---

[104] I Thessalonians 5:18
[105] Job 2:9
[106] John 3:16

for me when I turned twelve, when he thought it was time (two years was an eternity at age ten).

My parents taught me most of what I knew about prayer, and I wish they had taught me more. This is what I wish I had learned earlier: God is a not a genie in a bottle, at our disposal, to grant our every wish. God is a Father who develops His children through discipline. It is my responsibility to pray for and figure out God's will for my life.[107] It is in God's will for our lives that we find real peace and fulfillment. Just like there is a struggle with our parents, we will also struggle with the Lord as we work things out. And finally, we have an enemy who wants nothing more than to derail God's will for our lives.[108]

My Mother's Prayer

At twenty-three I took the big leap of faith to work for my brother's company in Houston, Texas. My main hesitation was that it was so far away from home and without friends or family there.

Before embarking on my big adventure, my mother confided her prayer for me. She said, "I pray you quickly find a church you like and make those people your family." She was a wise woman, for she knew that my faith would be vulnerable in a new world without a support system. She also knew of the possibility that I might find the wrong kind of support system.

My brother Joel was the largest shareholder in the company but had moved a year earlier to Colorado for an oil and gas consulting opportunity. One of his motivations for hiring me was so he would have eyes and ears on the inside.

---

[107] Romans 12:1-2
[108] I Peter 5:8

Randy and Debbie

Joel arranged for me to stay with our cousin for the first couple of days until I found a place to live.

I had never met our cousin Randy Boggs or his wife Debbie. My mother's sister, Annie Mae Halbert, moved to San Antonio twenty-five years before my birth. They hoped the drier climate would help their severely asthmatic child. Randy was her grandchild, making him my second cousin.

Nearing the outskirts of Houston, I pulled over to a phone booth, which now sounds so ancient to me. Randy was very friendly on the phone and gave me directions to his apartment.

Randy worked for my brother in Houston for about a year before Joel moved to Colorado. He grew up in San Antonio, went to school at Abilene Christian University, and was a Texan through and through, complete with cowboy boots and a big ole belt buckle. I would find out years later that Randy and Debbie were college friends with Max Lucado, the Christian author I admired.

At the time of this meeting, Randy and Debbie had been married a little over a year and lived in a small one-bedroom apartment. They welcomed their long-lost cousin with big smiles and handshakes. They made room in the closet and had already made their sofa into a bed.

After a little small talk, they asked if I would like a cup of coffee, and we talked into the night at their breakfast, lunch, and dinner table. We seemed to have lots of catching up to do.

We talked about my brother Joel, the high-riding entrepreneur, and about my Aunt Annie Mae and Uncle Karlton, who Randy called Grandma and Grandpa. I recalled my visit at age ten to San Antonio and wondered if Randy was one of the kids we played with.

A Godly Coincidence

Finally, the conversation turned to church. To establish some common ground, Randy asked me, "Do you know any ministers or evangelists west of the Mississippi River?" Now, that is a pretty broad question, but quite typical of a Texan.

"Yes, when I was a teenager, I met a minister at a youth retreat in Columbus, Mississippi," I said. "He was the keynote speaker for the event, and we shared a cabin together. He had a great message to the youth, and though I was only twelve, he reached out to connect with me and I became a fan." (For several years after the youth retreat, my father, who knew I liked this minister, would bring me audio tapes from conferences where he had spoken. I consider him my spiritual mentor.)

"His name is Lynn Anderson. Do you know him?" I asked.

Randy and Debbie looked at one another nonplussed. "Yes," Randy said, "I married his daughter!"

What are the chances of that being a coincidence? I mean, really, what are the odds of this happening? A boy from Alabama goes to a youth retreat, the only youth retreat I ever attended; and I meet and befriend a thirty-something-year-old minister from Abilene, Texas. My father would later go to another conference in Oklahoma and think to buy audio tapes from the conference which Anderson was a speaker.

Lynn Anderson's tapes would mentor me and shape my theology. Ten years later, I would move to Texas not knowing a soul, meet cousin Randy for the first time, and he is recently married to Mr. Anderson's daughter. I don't know about you, but I am suspicious of some divine orchestration here. It sounds like answers to my mother's prayers and answered prayer from the old farmhouse.

My New Family

This wild coincidence with Randy and Debbie made us fast friends. My Houston experience is unimaginable to me without this deep and important friendship. Randy and Debbie became a bridge to many of the foundational relationships I formed. A week after my arrival they took me to church with them. Randy and Debbie were new Houstonians, too, and Debbie's father, Lynn, recommended they visit Quail Valley Church of Christ. Lynn's endorsement intrigued me. There was no thought of being led by God. I was just going with the flow.

On Sunday, we go to the Quail Valley Church in Alief, Texas, off Interstate 59. The church known as *The Barn* met in a converted barn. The lingering appreciation of the '60s made it cool to me for church to meet in a barn. The church packed in their 200 or so members for services. The worship experience felt inspired and special.

After church, we went out to lunch with a group of twenty-somethings to eat authentic Tex Mex food, which would become a favorite. There, I met a young Englishman named Adrian Hall. He came to Houston by way of the Royal Navy. A recent convert to Jesus, he was looking for a roommate to defray expenses. Within days, we began negotiations to become roommates.

Within a week, I have new family in Randy and Debbie, and I have a new church family in Quail Valley Church and have lined up a new roommate in Adrian Hall.

Mother's prayer echoed in my ears. This church was to make a profound impact on my life and my thinking. The Holy Spirit was to become more than words on a page, but instead, the indwelling of God inside of me and the source of a lifelong, ongoing conversation. This changed me and is still changing me.

The Wild West

Starting my new job, I was going to need all the help I could get. On my first day in the office, I found the lead foreman lying drunk on his desk, with a handgun on the floor. He put three shots through the ceiling the night before. Wow, I was really in the Wild West!

Jim, my new boss, a 45-year-old former high-level accountant with U.S. Steel, had a fifth of Jack Daniels and a package of cocaine in his desk drawer, and a twenty-something Middle Eastern Muslim mistress in the shadows. I was getting a first-class education in business -- Texas-style.

Over the next eighteen months, I would spend a lot of time with the people in my company. We often worked long hours together, with plenty of time to absorb their worldview. I was also very engaged with this new family of Christian believers at Quail Valley. There was no doubt a huge dichotomy between the two groups. From one emanated life and enjoyable times. From the other not so much good other than the work we did.

Only now have I contemplated how I might have been different had I immersed myself in my work and my co-workers without my friends from Quail Valley. My mother's prayer may have been the thing that protected me from what I might have become.

Epilogue

We are told that college is supposed to prepare us and mold us, but it was nothing compared to the reshaping of the first years after college, when I felt the cuts and blows of the hammer and chisel.

But as painful as those years sometimes felt, I now realize all the shaping was going on in the hands of a caring Father. He was careful. When there was a major cut or blow, He was faithful to provide me comfort and encouragement with people like Randy and Debbie and other kind people from Quail Valley Church.

Discussion, Reflection, and Actionable Suggestions:

1. Have you been fortunate enough to have someone who loved you pray for you?
2. Do you have someone for whom you regularly pray? Have you seen God move on behalf of those prayers?
3. What may seem like unanswered prayer may be a learning experience or protection from God.
4. God is a Father who develops His children through discipline.
5. Have you ever experienced something that was beyond coincidence?
6. Do you think it was in God's will to answer the mother's prayer for the author?

15

Learning to Follow the Nudge of the Spirit

"So faith comes from hearing, and hearing through the word of Christ."
-- Romans 10:17

"DEAR LORD, LET ME TRUST that my good thoughts are from the Holy Spirit and help me to be obedient to His voice."

That was my prayer one Friday evening in 1982, in Houston, Texas. It would be a life changer.

Memoirs by Harry S. Truman

This book, *Memoirs by Harry S. Truman*, is important not because of the author's content, but because of the inscription written 30 years earlier. Inside the front cover is scrawled in faded ink: "To Clay, thank you so much. Jean Gustavson."

In 1982, with a sheepskin diploma still warm and a few career failures -- I mean, stepping stones behind me, I struck out 700 miles away from home. This was my go-west-young-man adventure into the real world. Surrounded by three million strangers in Houston, Texas, I am guided by my mamma's prayer: "Let him find a church quickly and make that his family."

Introduced to the Spirit of God

Not long after settling into my new job, apartment, and church, our church brought in a familiar face. Don Finto came to instruct us on how to hear the voice of God.

My first time to meet Don Finto was at the Belmont Church of Christ in Nashville, Tennessee. I was only thirteen years old and a guest of Wiley Dean. Wiley, a recent graduate of Middle Tennessee State University, had moved into my hometown to open a Kentucky Fried Chicken franchise.

Wiley invited me to an MTSU basketball game, and afterwards, introduced me to the Koinonia Bookstore in Nashville. There, we joined other youth to listen to a new genre of Christian folk music by a band called Dogwood. (I would later meet two of those band members again in Houston - Steve and Annie Chapman.)

The music was right down my alley. I was learning to play guitar and Dogwood's ballads reminded me of my favorite Eagles' songs. This was considered counter-culture for the time, since almost all Christian music was either hymns or gospel quartets. My Christian tradition forbade the use of musical instruments, so this music, for me, was borderline heretical. There was a little sign sitting on the piano in the bookstore. It read, "And whatever you do, do it heartily, as to the Lord, and not to men."[109]

The next morning, we went to church at Belmont Church of Christ. Don Finto was the minister there. The atmosphere was worshipful. I felt the presence of a gracious Spirit in the place and in his message. This experience would draw me back there for several years in a row for an annual pilgrimage.

---

[109] Colossians 3:17

An Experiment with Listening to the Spirit

Boy, it was a surprise to learn that Quail Valley invited Don Finto to tutor us on walking in the Spirit. This was the topic my father unwittingly squelched years earlier that caused many in our church to go their separate ways.

Don explained about learning to walk in the Spirit, "Your thoughts come from somewhere, don't they?" he said. To be honest, it never occurred to me where my thoughts came from. He continued, "Let's assume that they do come from somewhere. Let's also assume that good thoughts come from the Lord so we can obey them immediately. And that bad thoughts come from -- well, something other than God, and we will ignore those thoughts. And the thoughts we are unsure whether good or bad, we put on the shelf for later."

"This should be easy enough," I thought to myself. "I can do this." And so, I prayed, "Dear Lord, let me trust that my good thoughts are from the Holy Spirit and help me to be obedient to His voice."

The Day After and Reality

The next morning was Saturday and my day off. This was my day to do whatever I wanted to do. I rolled out of bed around 9:30, starving. I relished the vision of a big breakfast at McDonald's while walking from my apartment to the parking lot.

On the way, I pass a middle-aged woman taking a lamp up the steps to her apartment. A thought comes to me that says, "Ask the woman if you can help her unload her furniture." "Not right now," I argued with this thought. "I am starving, and she seems all right," I said to myself. "Okay," I thought, "you wanted to do this thing Don talked about last night," came the other voice in my head. "Okay, okay," I reluctantly agreed. "Ma'am," I said, "Could I help you move your furniture into your apartment?"

Don't we all have those conversations in our head? What would you call them, if not voices?

The lady turned and sighed, not speaking a word for the longest moment. Then, as the rest of her body drooped, and her shoulders slumped, she exhaled the words, "Would you?" "Sure," I said, as I walked to the small pull-behind U-Haul trailer.

There wasn't a lot to move, but because she lived on the second floor, it took us two hours to finish. As we passed on the sidewalk or in the hallway, I learned about her cancer and the death of her husband. She confided about her two twenty-something sons who were on drugs and stealing from her. She also said she was running from them and no one knew her new location.

By noon, my stomach was speaking to me in no uncertain terms. The cravings shifted from breakfast to a large supreme pizza. I looked for an exit opportunity when I heard the thought, "Ask her if you can buy her lunch." "No," was the resounding response from the other personality within me.

My Selfish Self

For the first time, the realization occurred to me there were two personality forces competing inside of me. "You have helped her all morning. She should offer to buy you lunch; you earned it. Let's go; forget about this woman. Enjoy what little you have left of your Saturday."

The other personality countered, "Remember what you said you wanted to follow. If you know it is good, obey immediately." "Okay, but I don't like it," selfish Clay grunted. "Mrs. Gustavson," I smiled, as if not having this conversation inside at all, "can I buy you lunch?" "Ohhh," she whispered, dragging out her muffled exclamation and letting it die slowly on her lips before a breathless "thank you" was expressed. She followed, "I don't have a job yet and my boys cleaned me out. I haven't eaten in a couple of days and I am starving."

On my way for pizza, I reflected on my Spirit-led experience. What the preacher didn't tell us the night before was how resistant my natural personality would be to God's leading.

What Following the Lead of the Spirit Can Accomplish

It was after stuffing ourselves with a large nine-topping pizza that Jean gave me her copy of *Memoirs by Harry S. Truman*. It had been her husband's. His father had fought in WWII just like mine and had been an admirer of Truman. I received her gift as something valuable because I knew it was precious to her.

Before leaving, there were a couple more good thoughts about Jean, and by now, I was tired of arguing with them. The first one was to give her one of the twenties I had in my wallet. The other was to ask her if she would be my guest at church in the morning. She said she would love to and we agreed upon a time and place to meet.

The next morning at the service, Jean Gustavson responded to the Lord. She asked Him to save her and lead her out of the mess she had found herself in.

I moved shortly after that and can't remember seeing Jean but a time or two after that morning. I hope and trust the Lord led others to Jean due to the magnitude of her need.

My Struggle with My Selfish Self

It would be great to report this incident was the beginning of a long and fruitful life of being sensitive to God's leading, and that I have been listening and following him every day. Honestly, I tried hard for a while, but I didn't keep up the intensity. The strength and selfishness of my natural personality caused me to realize just how selfish I am.

I abandoned trying to walk in the Spirit every day. It was just too exhausting and very inconvenient. The Lord was constantly having me do things that I didn't care to do. So, I stopped listening. I had rather do what I wanted to do rather than what the Lord wanted me to do.

Odd thing is, my unwillingness to listen is one of the reasons I have faith it is the voice of the Lord. If the thoughts were always something I wanted to do, I would suspect the thoughts are coming from my own selfish desires.

I am happy to announce that the Lord does continue to tempt me to do good and to follow His lead. The word *tempt* is a good word here because that is what it is like. He tempts me to respond to the Spirit of the Lord in a similar manner to how the devil tempts me to satisfy my flesh in illegitimate ways.

Another good thing that came from this is my natural personality became exposed for what it is. There is no need to defend it. It is very selfish.

Best of all, as I witnessed the good accomplished by following the Spirit, the more inclined I become to listen and obey. As the end of my days approach, my selfishness has turned into an advantage. Now I selfishly desire to be a part of what the Spirit is doing and accomplishing.

God Told Me So

In my Christian tradition, we did not have a God-told-me-so culture. Tradition was, once the last drop of ink dried on the book of Revelation, God stopped communicating. We could speak to Him, but He didn't speak back.

However, one of our strengths was that we valued scripture. We embraced the second of Martin Luther's five Solas: Sola Scriptura. We believed that every doctrine required scriptural authority.

The incident with Mrs. Gustavson was the start of learning to appreciate the God-told-me-so culture I find in some Christian groups. So, I began to look for the scripture to back up what I had experienced with Mrs. Gustavson. Next is what I discovered.

The Spoken Word of God

The Bible tells us that faith comes from hearing, and hearing through the word of Christ.[110] My tradition taught that faith comes from hearing or reading the Bible. I agree, that does build our faith. However, nowhere in the Bible does it foretell the assembling of a great new book that is to be our guide in all things. To the contrary, one of the main tenets of Jesus and the apostles' teaching is that He is sending His Spirit to indwell us, guide us, and teach us.[111] This more intimate method God uses to teach us complements the inspired writings.

There are two words in the Greek that are translated *word* into English. One is *logos* and the other is *rhema*.

The first, *logos*, refers principally to the total inspired Word of God and to Jesus, who is the living Logos. You can find the word *Logos* in John 1:1 and many other verses. The second Greek word translated *word* is *rhema*, which refers to the spoken word. *Rhema* literally means an utterance. You can find examples of the word *rhema* in Luke 1:38 and Acts 11:16.

Hearing the Lord's Voice

These two definitions of *word* in Greek allowed me to see Romans 10:17 in a new light. So, faith comes from hearing, and hearing through the (rhema, or utterance) of Christ.

---

[110] Romans 10:17

[111] Luke 11:13

Do you think my faith grew exponentially after this episode of hearing a specific instruction from the Spirit and seeing the amazing results? I know so. I heard and obeyed and "BAM" an incredible thing happened, and a life was changed. My faith in God soared.

Jesus said, "My sheep hear my voice, and I know them, and they follow me."[112] The word *voice* in the Greek is the word where we get our word for *phone*. It means sound, noise, voice, or language. "My sheep hear a voice -- words -- and when they hear them, they respond to them and follow My direction."

Again, it was Jesus who said, "Whoever is of God hears the words of God. The reason why you do not hear them is that you are not of God."[113]

According to Strong's Concordance, the word *hears* means to listen or to hear the voice of God that in turn gives birth to faith within. Again, the Greek word for *word* in this passage is *rhema*. In the latter part of this verse, Jesus says something very sobering and instructive. That is, it is instructive if a person will take it with the right attitude. Jesus says, "The reason why you do not hear the words of God is that you are not of God."

I Don't Hear from God

Some Christians tell me from time to time they don't hear from God. They are disturbed by the assertion that Christians should be hearing from God. Is it possible a person is hearing from God and doesn't realize it? It is possible they have the wrong vocabulary when it comes to the voice of God. Their spiritual lexicon may say, "I know this in my gut or in my heart," when, in reality, they are hearing from God.

---

[112] John 10:27

[113] John 8:47

If this troubles or concerns you, it might be you need to focus your awareness to the inner voice of God. For others, if you do not hear from God, it could be your wake-up call to seek a relationship with the Lord. It starts by first acknowledging Him as your King and putting your faith in Him to save you. There are other important instructions we get from the apostles, like making a public profession of our faith, both verbally and through baptism.[114][115] It is also important for our future growth and care to find and identify ourselves with a group of believers.[116]

The Lord may have led you to these verses today. His desire for all of us is to seek a relationship with Him. It is up to us to take the first step.

What the Prophets Have Said About the Spirit's Voice

Jesus foretells, as recorded by John in 16:13, "When the Spirit of Truth comes, He will guide you into all truth." The word *Spirit* in this verse is translated from the Greek word *pneuma*, meaning breath. When the "pneuma, or breath" of truth comes, He will be your guide into the whole truth.

The breath of the Spirit of God will guide us. The exciting possibility of being guided by the whispers of God magnifies the possibilities of our daily lives.

Jesus said about this possibility, "If you love me, keep my commands. And I will ask the Father, and He will give you another advocate or counselor to help you and be with you forever - The Spirit of Truth. The world cannot accept Him, because it neither sees Him

---

[114] Romans 10:9-10

[115] Acts 2:38

[116] Hebrews 10:25

nor knows Him. But you know Him, for He lives with you and will be with you."[117]

The early Christian prophet Paul had a lot to say about God whispering His instructions. Paul reminded his listeners, "Do you not know that you are a temple of God and that the Spirit of God dwells in you?"[118]

To be led by God, we must be able to hear instructions and discern their meaning. Again, Paul says, "For all who are led by the Spirit of God are sons of God."[119]

Sometimes the Lord's instructions are very practical and specific. An angel, or messenger, from the Lord told the early disciple Philip to go over to a chariot and stay near it. Philip obeyed, and upon meeting the Ethiopian eunuch in the chariot, Philip discovered the man reading from Isaiah 53. That passage just so happened to be about the betrayal and crucifixion of the Messiah. Philip explains the meaning of the passage, and moments later, Philip baptizes the eunuch into Christ as a new believer. All this because Philip heard and obeyed the voice of one he believed was sent from God.[120]

Believing the Lord is speaking to you and guiding you in various ways gives life so much more meaning and purpose. Though I believe in the voice of God, I am not arrogant about my ability to hear with perfect clarity. If you are like me, you don't always hear things from people with perfect clarity. Noise and distractions can confuse me, but I try my best to listen.

Over the years, I have matured and become more disciplined, but I still have plenty of selfishness and preoccupation with self-interest. Yet,

---

[117] John 14:15-17

[118] I Corinthians 3:16

[119] Romans 8:14

[120] Acts 8

I remain convinced (have faith) the Lord trusts me enough to speaks to me, and when I act, great things happen. These great things affect the Kingdom of God in exponentially positive ways. My belief is, they can for you too.

Discussion, Reflection, and Actionable Suggestions:

1. Have you ever considered where your thoughts come from?
2. Do you recall a time when you felt as if you heard the Lord speak to you?
3. Do you need to ask the Lord into your life, to be your Savior and King? If so, consider praying this prayer: Dear Lord, I want to turn my life around and follow you. I want you to be my King. I want to have your Spirit in me as my comforter and guide. Please lead me to like-minded people who will support my faith in you and help me to grow. In Jesus' Name.
4. Would you be willing to take the Don Finto challenge and obey your good thoughts as if they were coming to you from the Lord? If so, consider praying this prayer: Lord, I want to take the challenge of listening to you and obeying the promptings I receive from you. Help me to have an ear to hear and eyes to see. In Jesus' Name.

16

The Hem of Your Garment

And they begged that they may only touch the hem of His garment: and as many as touched were made perfectly whole.

-- Matthew 14:36

"PLEASE, LORD, IF YOU WOULD brush the hem of your garment over her, she will be healed."

Two Answered Prayers

Two closely related and connected prayers shaped my faith in God as a young man. The first one was a group prayer with my father, mother, sister, and two brothers.

It went like this: "Lord, we pray for mother; we believe her pain is real and reject that the doctors are saying that her problems are psychosomatic. We ask you to let us know what is wrong with her."

The second prayer went like this: "Lord, if you would brush the hem of your garment over her, she will be healed."[121]

My mother, Ruth Mize, started feeling bad before I left for Texas. She stopped working and stayed in bed most days. Mother complained

---

[121] Matthew 9:20

of serious pain in her lower back. She had gone to a couple of doctors, but none could find anything wrong with her. She was miserable, and we felt helpless.

One doctor told dad he thought her pain was psychosomatic. That was the cruelest of any possible diagnosis. It caused mother a lot of emotional pain and left the family with less empathy. My mother had always been the caregiver and had never feigned an illness in her entire life. Yet, the diagnosis of a doctor has a powerful influence. They are the trusted experts, and I am sad to say this incorrect diagnosis affected how we cared for her or didn't care for her.

Family Prayer

After six months at my new job in Houston, I went home for a visit. Mother was in bed most of the time. It was tiring to hear she had not improved. It was time to do something more.

We called a family prayer meeting. Mother seemed pleased that we were doing something. We all sat in a circle and held hands as we prayed for her. We prayed, "Lord, we pray for our mother; we believe her pain is real and reject that the doctors are saying that her problems are psychosomatic. Please let us know what is wrong with her."

A Long, Lovely Walk

After our prayer, mother seemed energized. She asked me to take a walk with her. This was a surprising suggestion. It was rare for her to get fully dressed. It thrilled me to spend this prized time together.

She laced up her tennis shoes, and we headed to the farm for a peaceful stroll on the winding gravel road. We walked, talked, and held hands. We talked about my adventure and about the future. Once, she bent over to pick up a stick in the road and threw it out of the way like she had plans to clean up the place. The real message we conveyed was how much we loved each other. For two miles, we had a respite from her pain. She felt bolstered that she had reinforcements and was weary of fighting without our full support.

On the Road Again

It was time for me to get on the road back to Houston. It was hard to leave her, but I was a tough young man, or at least that is what I told myself. The majority of my training was to be tough.

Back in Texas, it was business as usual. I was busy making new contacts in the oil and gas industry. For the week, my plan was a trip to Lake Charles, New Orleans, and ending up in Jackson to meet drilling engineers from Superior Oil, Marathon, and Amoco. On Monday, when speaking with Mother, she was optimistic about a new doctor's appointment in Birmingham.

The First Answer

On Thursday evening before leaving Jackson, going back to New Orleans, our office manager called and said to call my brother Gary. A vision flashed across my mind of my mother and father both lying in a casket. It was plain as walking into the parlor -- hair just in place, makeup, eyes closed, the hands. The hands always look strange -- too still and slender. Shaking my head to clear the thought, I called Gary.

"Clay, you need to come on to Birmingham. The doctor thinks he has found something that could be serious."

"What do you mean *serious*?"

"He thinks he has found a small cancer in her colon."

"How bad is it?"

"He is not sure, but thinks he found it early."

"Okay," I said, "I will be there as fast as this road will take me."

"No, take your time, be safe, but come on."

Finally, we are getting to the bottom of this, I thought. It must be a relief to mother to confirm that her problem is not psychosomatic. Within the week, God had answered our prayer. Maybe now we will all give her the unreserved support she has been needing.

Ironically, it was only a few hours later I found myself lying face down sobbing in the middle of St. Vincent's Hospital parking lot. Moments before, my brother told me the small cancer they detected was much more serious.

I drove from Jackson to Birmingham in record time, except for a brief stop in Tuscaloosa to shop for a new doll for mother. Times were hard for my mother's family during the Great Depression. She was one of 14 children. Her father's miscalculation on a commercial construction bid had bankrupted their well-to-do family. It sent them packing from their home in town to the country, where her brothers could help raise their food.

Mother was only four years old when this financial setback took place, and consequently, never received a doll. It was only a few months earlier that she had confided this story to me.

"Hmm, what a silly thought," she said, shrugging.

I will stop and buy her a doll, I thought. Maybe that will cheer her up.

Worse Than Expected

Unsuspecting, I walked into her hospital room. It was very quiet for 9:30 p.m. The lights were off except for some very dim indirect lighting in a corner of the room. My eyes had to adjust to see at all. The shadows signaled me there was more to the story than the earlier phone conversation while in Jackson.

Mother was lying on her side, with dad in the chair beside her. If I have one ability, it is to cheer my mother up. But that day, the room didn't brighten as I entered. I could have been an orderly coming by to change a pillow. I presented her with the doll. She gave me a half-smile and laid it on the nightstand, with only a minor examination.

It was obvious she was trying to rest, so I didn't stay long. As I watched the numbers above the elevator climb to the third floor, Gary and Linda rounded the corner. I knew by their faces I was about to hear bad news. "The cancer looks like it has spread to several organs."

"But you said only a trace was found in her colon."

"That was the original finding, but more showed up on the x-ray."

My heart felt heavy as lead. My essence drained out my feet into the elevator floor.

Face Down in Asphalt

Crestfallen, I slouched toward my car. The rest of the world did not understand the magnitude or significance of what was happening. Dropping to my knees, I then flopped on to my chest, face down before God in the parking lot.

"GOD, THIS IS **MY** MOTHER! YOU CAN NOT LET HER DIE," I screamed into the asphalt.

A strange sensation came over me as I laid there. I saw the Lord passing over my mother and the hem of his garment brushing over her. "Lord, if you would only brush the hem of your garment over her, she will be healed," I prayed.

In my mind, I heard these words: "Your mother will be okay." Peace flooded me. It felt good and warm like a tranquilizer. Then I heard the voice again. "But it doesn't mean she's healed." Even with the elucidation, the peace remained. It was a peace that passed my understanding.

For some incomprehensible reason, my mother's dire situation, like the old hymn proclaims, was *well with my soul*. The Lord spoke to me, and though the answer should have been anathema to me, instead it calmed my storm. As I look back, the peace that remained gave me confidence I was hearing from God and that He cared.

The next day, I would weep again after the exploratory surgery, when the doctor spoke to our family. He said, "There is nothing I can do. The cancer is too bad, and surgery will do her no good, so I simply sewed her back up. She will not last long." Openly, I wept, but not in desperation. I wept for what she was losing and for what we were losing.

God's Strategic Mercy

After picking myself up from the asphalt in the parking lot, I rented a room for the night. The key fit perfectly into the lock at the Red Roof Motor Inn on 20th Street in downtown Birmingham. My every move felt exaggerated and in slow motion. The deadbolt turned in Room 10B, in this ultra-modern room; that is, if you were living in the 50's. The room was lonely and felt like walking back in time, with a dated bedspread, a wrought iron hanging lamp, shag carpet, and paneled walls.

I had never been this alone in my life. I had to get out of the room. As fate would have it, across the street from my cheap hotel, my high school girlfriend was a cocktail waitress in the Ramada Inn lounge. If anyone could understand what I was losing, she would. She took time between customers as I filled her in on the details. She knew just what to say, and her compassion was evident. She truly comforted me. It was as if the Lord positioned her there just for me.

There were no tears when pillowing my head that night. My mind continued replaying the flowing garment of Jesus slightly brushing across my mother. Mother will be okay. There was still a warmth inside.

My request was made, and the answer came. He was guarding my mind and my heart. We will all be okay.

The End

Mother made it for two weeks, until May of 1982. We buried her on Friday, and Mother's Day was Sunday. My number two brother was with her when she passed. He said, as she drew her last breath, she opened her eyes wide like something big was taking place and then breathed her last. At that very moment, a fire alarm went off in the hospital and pandemonium broke loose. The universe was acknowledging the passing of a great person.

My brother who was with her was the one who most needed that special moment with her. It was God's grace to him. He believes she communicated to him through a song on the radio on the way home. It gave him peace. Though my oldest brother lived in Colorado, he made an impromptu visit ten days before the surgery. They made peace with their differences of opinion that led to hurt feelings a few years earlier. It seemed like God's grace to him.

I thank God for the miraculous recovery she made the day we walked hand in hand for two miles. Two weeks before, she was too sick to attend her mother-in-law's funeral. On this day, I couldn't tell anything was wrong. It was sublime.

The Lord's words to me, His acts of special kindness, and the peace I could not explain, all shaped my faith in His goodness. He proved again to be a kind Father to me.

Epilogue

During my mother's funeral, I was still surprised with this unusual calm and peace that remained. As the youngest child of older parents, I was more keenly aware of their mortality, and this had been a day I dreaded my whole life. Instead of horror, I am at peace.

I had complete confidence my mother was with the Lord. A verse came to me as I sat there: O death, where is your sting?[122] I chuckled to myself as I thought, I can laugh in the face of death and say, Is this all you've got?

Discussion, Reflection, and Actionable Suggestions:

1. Have you ever heard a whisper from the Lord that gave you peace?
2. Has the Lord ever given you special moments with a friend or family member just prior to their passing?
3. Can you recall a time of special kindness from the Lord?
4. Have you ever had a peace that you could not understand?

---

[122] I Corinthians 15:55

17

My Guardian Angel

Are not all angels ministering spirits sent to serve those who will inherit salvation?
-- Hebrews 1:14

BUSINESS BEGAN TO BOOM back in Houston, and the week after mother's death I found myself on a Superior Oil offshore drilling platform. We were forty miles into the Gulf of Mexico in the Cameron Block, off the Louisiana shore. This was the diversion I needed. We hung 200 feet above the waves, with a 360-degree view of the ocean. At night, the only light was the moon, the stars, and tiny flaring gas wells dotting the horizon. The earth seemed vast, and I felt small.

The next week we started a land job near Lake Charles for Amoco Oil. I would meet my guardian angel there. Losing consciousness, with both hands dripping blood, my prayer was simple and desperate: Lord, please help me.

My Days as a Roughneck

One of my duties as an oilfield salesman was that sometimes it required me to do double duty as a roughneck. Roughneck is the name given to men working with oilfield drilling equipment. The name is fitting.

Our company served oil companies who were actively seeking new oil by drilling wildcat wells. A wildcat well is a speculative endeavor, with hopes of hitting a gusher. Little is known about the oil and gas potential prior to drilling the wildcat.

Once a wildcat hits pay dirt, our company went to work. Our secret weapon was a Hewlett-Packard instrument probe attached to an electrical wire-line we lowered into the hole. The probe could measure both pressure and temperature and relay it by electrical impulse to our equipment topside.

The oil and gas engineers could take the data and calculate the size of the underground reservoir of oil or gas. We provided the intelligence they needed to plan the location of future wells.

The Wildcat

This wildcat well, located outside Lake Charles, punctured a pasture a half mile off a paved road. Amoco built a gravel road out to the site, and once at the site, they built a large wooden platform around the wellhead. The wooden platform's design kept workers like us off the ground and out of the mud created by dirt and rock fragments pouring out of the hole. Drilling an oil well is a muddy business.

The road came right up to the wooden platform, where eight cars parked at the platform's edge. Several pieces of machinery sat on the platform, ready when needed, and moved into place with a portable crane. The well was forty yards from our parked cars.

There were twelve people there in total -- seven from our company and five from Amoco.

One of the Guys

Our company had very capable roughnecks with lots of experience. I had very little experience and a college degree. Both were a disadvantage when working with roughnecks. The roughnecks assumed you felt entitled and stood determined to make sure you realized you knew nothing about their business. The pecking order was well established around the rig, and I was plainly the scrawniest chicken.

This was nothing new for me. This was normal, growing up the youngest of four brothers. The experience was the same on the football field and with other men around the farm and manufacturing plants in Alabama. What was needed to win these guys over was to establish myself by showing them my willingness to do whatever was needed.

We pulled our wire-line truck on the platform to assemble our ten-foot joints of lubricator pipes onto the wellhead. One of the reasons a good roughneck is so valuable around a drilling rig is that the area around a wellhead is very dangerous.

The location for a wildcat well is chosen because a geologist identifies a dome-shaped area in the strata of the rock formation below. This dome, he hopes, is the result of a large amount of natural gas causing pressure and pushing with such force that it creates a dome-like formation in the rock.

You can imagine the pressure it would take to push up on the formation layer that has 6,000 feet of dirt on top of it. Picture a huge champagne bottle.

The equipment on the surface of the well is extremely heavy-duty to control that kind of pressure. These regulators at the surface, called blow-out preventers, can handle as much as 25,000 psi, or pounds per square inch, of pressure. If not assembled correctly, this mega force will toss the ten-foot links of thick steel pipe into the air like matchsticks. Anyone unlucky enough to get caught standing in the wrong place when they fall back to earth is dead.

My Mistake

As our truck backed into place at the wellhead, I noticed a 55-gallon drum sitting between the wire-line truck and the wellhead. It needed to be cleared, so I jumped into action.

The drum was originally filled with grease. The top was missing, and the barrel was about half full of water from the consistent rainfall the past week. With the water in it, it weighed about 150 pounds. My idea was to grab the barrel, jerk it onto its bottom rim, and roll it away.

What was unknown to me was the barrel was initially opened by a giant can opener. Just inside the open barrel rim hid jagged metal. Grabbing the barrel, I gave it a yank and rolled it away so that the truck could back up to do its work. Not realizing what was happening, I looked down to see my slashed hands bleeding. The open gashes filled with mud and grease. My first thought was embarrassment, but I quickly made two fists and hoped nobody would notice what happened.

Stepping back behind the crew, I observed as a few crew members began preparing the wellhead. After a couple of moments, I looked at the platform below my balled-up fists, and I could see blood pooling up. Sweat broke out on my face and neck in the cool morning air.

Inconspicuously, I made my way through the machinery and back to the parked cars. I felt light-headed and knew I needed a seat fast.

My Guardian Angel

Finding my truck, I sat down. My head was spinning, and as it seemed I might lose consciousness, I whispered, "Lord, help me."

About that time the passenger door opened. Scooting in was a young man. He was dressed in khaki pants, a white shirt, and standard work boots like a company man. He was under thirty, with blond hair, tall and athletic. His demeanor was professional. He didn't say anything; he just reached and took my hand, opened it up, and began cleaning out the mud and grease. Finally, he put something on the wounds and bandaged both hands with gauze.

Sitting with my head back and eyes closed, I tried to keep from passing out. When he finished, he simply got out and closed the door.

Within thirty minutes, the sweating stopped, my breathing returned to normal, and the blood came back into my face. A few minutes later I felt like I could go back to the well site.

Looking for My Angel

I wanted to thank the kind man who had bandaged my hands. Seven people at the site worked for my company, so that left five possible men. Approaching each man from Amoco one at a time, I couldn't find him.

No one knew who I was talking about as I described the man. No one knew him, and no one fit the description. From that moment on, I believed I had met my guardian angel.

Angelic Research

Emma Heathcote, a 22-year-old graduate of theology from Birmingham University, UK, conducted a very interesting research project on angel encounters. After placing advertisements in newspapers and religious magazines requesting accounts of "angel experiences," she has collected hundreds of testimonies. Her research shows that regardless of religious faith, including atheists, people report similar experiences. If you would like to learn more about her research, go to http://www.share-international.org/archives/angels/ang_gfencounters.htm.

Angels Among Us

Many people believe they have encountered angels. In my case, the person, or being, did not do anything seeking recognition for their deed. It makes me wonder how many times we encounter angels unaware.

Growing up in rural Alabama, it was not unusual for a door-to-door salesman to show up uninvited, essentially a stranger. My mother always took time to visit with them and hear what they had to say, and she would often buy from them. She always seemed to go out of her way, showing these people hospitality, giving them tea or Cokes with a snack.

Once, it occurred to me to ask her about this, and she paraphrased a Bible verse for me. "Always show hospitality to strangers," she said, "because you never know when you may entertain angels."[123]

One day, I called out in distress to the Father, and an unexplained person showed up to help me. Whoever he was, he was *my* angel.

Discussion, Reflection, and Actionable Suggestions:

1. Have you ever thought you had an angel encounter?
2. The Bible says we may be unaware we are entertaining angels. Will that awareness affect the way you treat strangers?

---

[123] Hebrews 13:2
Other References
Psalms 50:15
Matthew 18:10

18

A Painful Learning Curve

How much better is it to get wisdom than gold, and to get insight rather than silver.
-- Proverbs 16:16

"DEAR LORD, EVERY ROAD seems to be a dead end. Please give me wisdom."

A journey. A prayer. A series of failures. What appears to be dead ends and poor decisions can instead be nothing more than an unpleasant but beneficial learning curve.

Have you prayed for something and you didn't get it? Or at least it didn't look like you got it. Have you ever prayed for something and it seemed like all hell broke loose? Have you ever prayed for something and the journey to receiving it seemed too long and hard?

God and Our Goal Setting

Our prayers are at times in conflict with the Lord's plans for our life. Obviously, if He made us and has a purpose for our existence, then our arbitrary plans and prayers for our life are most likely inferior, if not contrary, to God's plans.

He said to Jeremiah, "'I know the plans I have for you,' says the Lord."[124] If the Lord knew the plans He had for Jeremiah, then He knows the plans He has for us.

Here is a good prayer for any of us: Lord, teach me the plans you have for my life. Teach me to set my sights on your goals for me. Show me how I resist you and help me to stop it. Teach me and give me the strength to work in symphony with you, in order to see your plans accomplished.

A Prayer for Wisdom

The Lord met with Solomon and requested he ask for whatever he would, and He would give it to him. This was Solomon's response: Give me wisdom and knowledge, that I may lead this people, for who is able to govern this great people of yours?[125]

My mother told me this story about Solomon one night as she sat by my bed. That night, I began to pray, "Lord, please give me wisdom."

Here is wisdom:

> *Trust in the Lord with all your heart, and do not lean on your own understanding. In all your ways, acknowledge him, and he will make straight your paths (Proverbs 3:5-6).*
>
> *If any of you lacks wisdom, let him ask God, who gives generously to all without reproach, and it will be given him. But let him ask in faith, with no doubting, for the one who doubts is like a wave of the sea that is driven and tossed by the wind (James 1:5-6).*

---

[124] Jeremiah 29:11
[125] II Chronicles 1:10

Two Kinds of Wisdom

The scripture tells us there are two kinds of wisdom. The kind that comes from above and the kind that comes from below. Later in the chapter, we will look at a gauge for testing where our wisdom is coming from -- above or below.

There are a lot of powerful people that operate out of wisdom from below. They are wise in the eyes of the world. Many of these worldly-wise people act as role models for our young people. They are often rich and impressive.

I believe a great deal of my early struggles as a young man came because of the war between these two types of wisdom. I wasn't wise enough to know what to want or what to pray for. Knowing the wise thing to pursue for my life eluded me. I looked around to the wisdom of the world and did what they were doing. There was definitely a preoccupation with making money.

Did you have a truly wise person teach you how you should pray and help you make wise choices for your life based on how the Lord has gifted you? Wouldn't that be great? Would we have listened if we had?

How do we determine if the wisdom we are getting is from above or below? Can we put wisdom to the spiritual test? Are we attracted to the wisdom from above or below?

Wisdom from Above

How do we know if wisdom's origin is from above or below? James, the brother of Jesus, tells us:

> *The wisdom that is from below is envious, selfish, or self-seeking, engenders confusion, and produces evil, while that which is from above is pure, peaceable, gentle, willing to yield,*

> *full of mercy, and good fruits, without partiality and hypocrisy, and it produces righteousness (James 3:16-18).*

Look at these adjectives again for wisdom from below. They are envious, selfish, causes confusion, and creates evil. What is the focus of this type of wisdom? Self. I. Me. Self-seeking. Selfishness. To focus on self is to operate in wisdom from below.

James continues:

> *Where do those fights and quarrels among you come from? They come from your selfish desires that are at war in your bodies, don't they? You want something but do not get it, so you commit murder. You covet something but cannot obtain it, so you quarrel and fight. You do not get things because you do not ask for them! You ask for something but do not get it because you ask for it for the wrong reason—for your own pleasure. You adulterers! Don't you know that friendship with the world means hostility with God? (James 4:1-4).*

What is the focus of wisdom from above? The adjectives are pure, peaceable, gentle, willing to yield, full of mercy, and good fruits, without partiality and hypocrisy. Notice they are all about how to relate to others. Wisdom from above is others-focused.

Another Failure

After two years in Houston, the business failed, as did thousands in Houston, New Orléans, Oklahoma City, and Denver. Oil went from $105 a barrel to $40 a barrel. OPEC had decided to flex its muscle. I bought a house in a new development, and within a few short months, the unsold new houses in my neighborhood were selling for $40,000 less than my mortgage. Not good.

When I moved to Houston, people were pouring into Houston at a rate of 30,000 a month. Now people were leaving at the same rate.

Commercial real estate companies built sixty-story high rises and demolished them before anyone ever moved in because there was no one to move in. Without a job, I walked away from my house, giving it to my roommate, hoping he could find a roommate to help him keep up the mortgage. I went back to my hometown and moved in with my dad, who was learning to be a widower. A few months later, my old roommate told me he walked away from the house, leaving it empty and me still on the mortgage.

Had the Lord led me down the wrong path? Had He led me into an ambush? Could I call Him faithful?

Never Judge God

Here is a lesson: Never judge God. Never judge God, and especially on another person's experience. We may look at someone's life and think the Lord is not faithful to them. The truth is, we have no idea what is going on.

It would be easy to look at my experience in Houston as a colossal failure, but I don't. My experience in Texas was a great entrepreneurial adventure. I was brave and felt like a pioneer as I learned how to manage a large city. A new church and new people challenged my theology and forced me to grow. And I grew as a business person, because doing business with Fortune 100 companies like Exxon and Mobil caused me to mature and step up my game.

My faith grew when my salary was discontinued, and I saw the Lord provide for me time and again, and often in the nick of time. Lifelong friends were made in people, such as my co-worker Walter Blanchard, who became like a brother. Jim Bevis, my minister at Quail Valley, and I would eventually move back to Florence, Alabama, where we would deepen our friendship. We would one day serve together on the Promise Keepers board of directors, and he would later recruit me into the Florence Rotary Club. Randy and Debbie Boggs, my cousins who took me in when I first moved to Houston, remained great friends.

My return to my hometown to live with my dad was not with my tail tucked and defeated. Instead, I came back full of confidence to embark on my next venture -- that would, incidentally, end in failure. I was in the arena and battling every day. I was bloody, but I was learning, growing, and getting stronger and smarter. Things that didn't work, I was learning to avoid. I was losing my naiveté.

Prayers from the Farmhouse

Though I could attribute a lot of that life-transforming experience to many things, I keep going back to the old farmhouse with the prayer rug and chair. Memories remain of me pouring out my issues to God and asking for His help. Like all great adventures, mine had danger, fear, and failure. It also had thrills, development, and awakening, and I am convinced the Lord heard my prayers, sent help, and cleared a path for me.

> *Trust in the Lord with all your heart, and do not lean on your own understanding. In all your ways acknowledge him, and he will make straight your paths (Proverbs 3:5-6).*

My conviction is, be careful not to judge what the Lord is doing. What looks like failure to an outsider could be hands-on training from the Lord. What looks like a painful experience to an outsider may be an exhilarating adventure to the one going through it.

Just because an endeavor fails, doesn't mean that it was not one of the most valuable experiences of your life. It is in these experiences that we uncover hints to the themes God weaves through our lives like connecting threads. Isolated events can seem to have no rhyme or reason, but taken together, a theme becomes faintly visible and a clue to our destiny. God is bigger than what happens to us, bigger than our failures, bigger than our losses. He works it all together for not only our good, but it is a part of the creative process to create an authentic person -- a member of His family. These failures are not only valuable, they are essential!

During the process of all of this, the thing we forget is that we are in a battle. Battles are not fruitless. They are strengthening and illuminating. As iron sharpens iron, so can a battle sharpen a man or woman. The journey to our answers may require a series of failures to teach us, toughen us, and get some things out of our system.

The quicker we learn how to pray and what to pray for, the more wisdom from above will guide our life, and our decisions will produce things that are pure, peaceable, gentle, willing to yield, full of mercy and good fruits, without partiality or hypocrisy.

My human nature doesn't like the idea of being obedient. It takes me back to being a kid. My father didn't like for me to ask why when he told me what to do. And I hated, "Because I said to."

This changed when I realized that the Lord's commands were not to be done *just because He said so*, but because they were the keys to living an abundant life. Why do we resist what is in our best interest? How long does it take for us to learn to trust the One who has our best interest at heart?

Discussion, Reflection, and Actionable Suggestions:

1. Is it possible that some of your prayers conflict with the Lord's plan for your life?
2. Are you going through a time where leaning on your own understanding leads to despair?
3. Trusting the Lord is bigger than your circumstances is a choice and a decision. Are you willing to trust in the Lord to work

through your circumstances to teach you and work them for your good?

4. Are you willing to pray this prayer: Lord, teach me the plans you have for my life. Teach me to set my sights on your goals for me. Show me how I resist you and help me to stop it. Teach me how to work in symphony with you to see them accomplished.
5. Have you been more in tune to the wisdom from below than the wisdom from above?
6. Are you guilty of judging God? Do you need to confess and repent of that?
7. Are you willing to ask the Lord to give you understanding about some of the failures in your life and how He has used them to develop you into the person He wants you to be?

19

I Don't Want This Business Anymore, You Can Have It

In all thy ways acknowledge him, and he shall direct thy paths.
-- Proverbs 3:6

"LORD, I DON'T WANT THIS business anymore. You can have it, because I don't want it. I will work for you and do whatever it is that you would like for me to do. I will work here until the doors close, and then I will find another job."

Another New Venture

In 1987, I launched my own business out of a spare bedroom. The reason was because I didn't want to move, and the Humana Corporation was transferring me to Huntsville. My new business was providing employee benefits to small and growing companies. Within a year, I formed a partnership to expand our expertise and take advantage of the economies created. John, my new partner, and I met previously when he provided me with introductory training on a line of financial products.

A year earlier John, too, had launched his own business as a financial planner. We agreed to form a corporation, share expenses, and hopefully create synergy. Together, we moved to real commercial office space in a developing area of town.

We began to grow, and we added an experienced office manager and three additional associates. One associate was an old pro, another had some experience and a big upside, and the other was new and in need of grooming. We now had five producers contributing to our overhead. Financially, the future looked bright. We each had different skills we brought to the organization. John had great training skills for bringing on more new associates. Jack, our old pro, had a lot of marketing ideas. Brenda loved to open new cases, and I was good at connecting with potential new clients.

Our Own Office Building

An old friend, Bill, saw our growth and approached me about buying an old but stately building in the downtown business district. His father once occupied the building and was motivated to sell. It was a great location and an ideal place to create a stable business presence in the community. The building had a total of 7,000 square feet of office space, with 3,000 square feet already occupied. The rent coming in from the anchor tenant would service the debt required to buy the building. This seemed like a no-brainer to me. My partner and I agreed that we would buy the building.

It would be two months until we could get all the paperwork complete and finalize the closing. Little did I know that my partner and his wife were discussing divorce. A week prior to the close, John broke the news to me. "I am exhausted mentally and emotionally," he said. "The way things are working out with Donna and I, I don't feel comfortable going through with the purchase."

Though I hesitated, I still felt confident in the future and told John that I would go ahead with the purchase without him. We agreed the corporation could simply rent our space from me. This would accomplish the same thing, except instead of us being on the hook together, I was going it alone. He agreed, and we proceeded.

To the Brink of Failure Again

I underestimated the toll the divorce would take on John's productivity and income to the firm. We needed his production to cover our regular expenses, plus the additional expenses associated with moving. His extreme slowdown in income was the first nail in what was beginning to look like my coffin.

Wave two came after we were in our new building for two months. Jack, our old pro, came into my office with pictures. These were not just any pictures, but pictures of his wife with another man. Of course, this was a personal tragedy for Jack, and we had just witnessed the business impact divorce had on John and his production. We would witness a repeat of this with Jack. He lost his motivation to work as the divorce drug on, and he eventually moved out of our office.

Wave three came a couple of months after Jack's revelation. Brenda comes in with good news. "I'm pregnant," she says beaming. "We are so excited and have decided to take time off to prepare for the baby." Well, I am excited for her, but not for me. We needed her to help pay the firm's bills.

So now it is down to John at 50%, our associate Sam who needs training, our office manager, and myself. My time is needed to bring in new clients, so Sam's much needed training gets pushed to the side. Unfortunately, Sam's career with us becomes a casualty of the situation.

A week after Brenda leaves, my office manager Jenny, who has been taking night classes, knocks on my door. "Clay," she says, "I could not get my classes at night this semester, so I need to take off on Tuesdays and Thursdays."

Knowing this would put us in a double bind, I balked. "No way we can run a business with our office manager out two days of the week. We can't cover for you with all that is going on here. I am sorry, but I can't allow that." With that, she stood, picked up her purse, threw down a book by Og Mandino I suggested she read, and walked out the door. That is the last time I ever saw her.

I still held out some hope that John would get through his ordeal and that we could rebuild again. I thought we could do it if we could just hang on for a while longer. Then the big wave five hit. John came in my office and said, "I have decided to go back to law school. I have wanted to do this for a long time, and I have decided to do it. I am sorry to leave you hanging."

I Give Up

After he walked out, I was sitting all alone in my 7,000 square foot building completely dejected. This endeavor had gone south fast. It would be a matter of days now until I put the building up for sale, closed the doors, and tried to find a job.

Sitting alone at my desk, I decided to pray. "Lord, I don't want this business anymore. You can have it, because I don't want it. I will work for you and do whatever it is that you would like for me to do. I will work here until the doors close, and then I will find another job."

New Ownership

The next week's schedule had me go to Cleveland, Ohio, to train for a new company. This opportunity was to represent the Ohio company as an independent recruiter and trainer for their small group health insurance product. There was a little money left in the account, and I didn't know what to do yet, so I went.

After returning home, it was day to day. The expectation was that any day the lack of funds would force me to close the doors. Weeks went by and then months, but it never happened. I never borrowed money, and the funds never dried up. I continued to work for what was now the Lord's business. Little by little, the partnership between myself and the company in Cleveland flourished beautifully. For the next seventeen years, the business grew every single year. Working for the Lord's company turned out to be such a blessing and a real joy.

The more successful we became, the more I would catch myself taking credit for our accomplishments. Let me set the record straight here. The business was failing when I owned it, and it prospered when He owned it. This experience shaped the way I think. Giving my business to the Lord was a very profitable business decision.

This episode also shaped my faith in the Lord. Now I usually say a little prayer before most every endeavor. I say, "Lord, you know I can't do this without you. I need your help, and if it is not to be, let it fail quickly. If I am to be successful in this, I need you to anoint me to do this. Amen." I have experienced many quick failures, but I am also amazed at how many ideas have flowed to me at just the right moment to accomplish the things that have presented themselves for me to do.

The Lord answered my prayer to take my business and allowed me to work for Him under the new ownership. He is a great owner to work for, and He truly blesses His employees.

Epilogue

Within ten years, my house and office building were paid off, and I was debt free. My staff grew to four and were very competent to serve over a hundred independent contractors we recruited and trained. So much of the business success was due to the diligence and attentiveness the staff paid to those we served.

My position with the company required -- rather, allowed -- me to travel for the company to do seminars, workshops, and attend conventions. Fortunately, these conventions hailed from the most beautiful locations in the world, with professionally-planned opportunities I would unlikely do for myself.

Then, as if it were time, the business began to turn in a different direction. Things changed -- the market changed, and within a year or two, there was no business. In those last two years, the market that existed became very frustrating to deal with. The frustration prepared me to move on. The years of plenty were over, and the years of famine arrived. I understood what Joseph experienced in Egypt.

Also, like Joseph, I have not suffered during the famine.[126] The early lean years taught me to live a conservative lifestyle.

The decline of the business was as if the Lord was helping me change the emphasis of my life from financial pursuits to joyful pursuits. There was an adjustment going from an excellent paycheck to a very modest one. But, I was set free to pursue a higher calling. Now the decision-making process is less about financial rewards and more about the joy it brings myself and others.

Sometimes I need to pinch myself. It is hard to believe I get to use my strengths and gifts to do things I enjoy. I may not travel or go on the vacations I once did, but I wouldn't go back. I am happy with this simple life. It is as if I had help all along the way.

Discussion, Reflection, and Actionable Suggestions:

1. Are your circumstances such that it feels like your whole world is crumbling and you are ready to give up?
2. Are you willing to let go and give your circumstances to the Lord?

---

[126] Genesis 41

3. If you are, join me in this prayer: Dear Father, I give up. It is more than I can do and more than I can bear. Please take it and do with it what you will. I will go and do whatever you like. I turn my life over to you for your leading and guidance.

20

The Wayward Wife

She will chase after her lovers but not catch them; she will look for them but not find them. Then she will say, "I will go back to my husband as at first, for then I was better off than now."

-- Hosea 2:7

"**M**Y WIFE IS HAVING an affair."

The book of Hosea is a story about an adulterous wife who eventually comes back to her husband. It is a true story that serves as an allegory about God's wife, Israel. The following is another true story, with an unusual twist, as God answers a prayer of resignation. This dramatically-timed answer shaped my faith too.

Out of the blue one day, a friend said, "My wife is having an affair."

"What?" I asked.

"Yes, I think Mitzi is having an affair."

"You said *think*."

"I don't know for sure, but it just now occurred to me that she is having an affair. Her odd behavior lately just adds up to she is having an affair."

"Do you know who with?"

"Yeah, her boss, John."

The Confirmation

A week later, Bill told me he tapped his home phone, and sure enough, the recordings confirmed their affair. He learned the affair wasn't a casual one. It was intimate and deeply emotional, despite her boss' obligations to a wife and four children.

Bill has the disposition of a bulldog. Once he bites down, he is single-minded in his focus. He confronted them, and they agreed to stop the affair. However, Mitzi was not open to leaving her job. She temporarily convinced Bill it was important to keep up appearances to protect John's wife from learning of their affair. He agreed, though he knew that if she continued working with him, she could not break her emotional ties. Though more discreetly, Mitzi continued the affair with the man she had fallen in love with.

He tried everything to win her back. He began to court her again. He brought her flowers and gifts and took her on vacations and began a conversation about children.

He also boosted the intensity of his spiritual life. He became earnest with church attendance, Bible study, and prayer. He found a Christian counselor and encouraged her to join him.

When this approach didn't produce quick results, Bill threatened he was going to expose the affair to John's wife. This threat extremely distressed Mitzi, and she agreed to quit the job. Though Bill won this small battle, he was losing the bigger battle as Mitzi's resentments grew. Though he couldn't prove it, he knew their affair had not stopped, and he knew her well enough to know she was protecting John and their relationship.

After she quit the job, not only did the affair not stop, it escalated. Months drug on as Bill tried one thing and then another to either win Mitzi back, or in some way, manipulate her to stop the affair.

When he called to give me updates, I began to wonder if his motivation was love or stubbornness. From a spiritual standpoint, I admired him for his commitment to his vows, but from a practical standpoint, I wondered if his motivations had become obsessive and unhealthy.

Downhearted, he decided to expose the affair to John's wife, Jessica. He knew this was a drastic measure that would initially push Mitzi farther away, but he felt he was at the end of his rope. Bill paid Jessica a visit and disclosed the affair. Her reaction was not unlike Bill's. She was not about to give up her family without a fight. Not only did she have a husband to fight for, but four young children.

This was the straw that caused Mitzi to move out on her own. She no longer had a need to keep up appearances of a marriage with Bill, so she got her own apartment.

But Bill thought that with John out of the way, he stood a chance to mend the relationship with his wife. Persistently, he attempted to woo her with notes and gifts. She responded with petulance, and the more he reached out to her, the angrier she became.

John and Mitzi's affair was stymied, but they found creative ways to slip away for intimate moments. After a few more months of having his advances rebuffed, Bill decided divorcing Mitzi might be the better way to get her attention. He was chasing the wind, desperately trying to engineer something in hopes to shift her feelings toward him.

The Divorce

Bill had divorce papers served. She had no objection to this and was quite willing to move forward with the divorce. Disappointed by her reaction, Bill hatched a new idea. He would give her everything they had worked for together.

Again, Mitzi was unmoved. Not only was she not moved, but this gesture made her more indignant. In her mind, it was just another selfish ploy to guilt her to come back. Unfazed, she took everything in the divorce and never looked back.

Giving Up and the Prayer

All of this transpired over about a two-year period. I didn't know all the details, but Bill called me every month or so with an update and to talk. He called one evening, and I sensed his discouragement. He sounded resigned. He said, "I think I will give up."

I said, "Are you really serious about giving up?"

"Yes, I am. I'm tired."

"Well, thank God, you have been needing to do that for a long time."

"Yeah, I guess you are right. It is hopeless."

"Are you ready to let go of this relationship? Are you willing to turn her over to the Lord and let Him deal with her as He wants?"

"Yes, I am."

"Do you mind if I say a prayer for you and for Mitzi?"

"Sure, go ahead."

"Father," I prayed, "thank you for loving us and hearing our prayer. Thank you that Bill is ready to release Mitzi over to you. Let her see the truth about her life and this relationship. Allow her to see the truth about what she is doing. In Jesus' Name. Amen."

We talked for another twenty minutes before a beep let him know he had another call waiting on the other line. He said, "Excuse me, and let me see who this is calling me."

"Sure," I said.

A moment later, he came back on the line. "Clay, I have to go. This is Mitzi on the other line, and she is crying. I will call you later."

An Unlikely Answer

A few days went by, and I tried to call him several times, but all the calls went to voicemail. I couldn't imagine what happened. Why would Mitzi call Bill crying? She had been so cold and emotionless, except for outbursts of anger.

Finally, he called me. "You are not going to believe what happened," he began. "About the time you were praying, John's wife Jessica walked in on Mitzi and John at Mitzi's apartment. She destroyed Mitzi's apartment. She broke all her dishes and most everything in the apartment. Then she started in on Mitzi. She beat her up pretty good. She punched and clawed her several times in the face and pulled a big handful of her hair out. The revealing part is that Bill didn't raise a hand to stop it. He just watched as Jessica pummeled her."

"The crazy thing is," he continued, "in the middle of being punched in the face, she confided she called out my name to help her. That told her something about who really loved her, and we have been together every minute since I picked her up that night."

Understanding How God Works Is a Mystery

There is no denying the impact this episode had on me as I witnessed an unusual and dramatic answer to my prayer at the request of my friend.

Why the Lord responded so quickly remains a mystery to me. Was it just perfect timing, or was it a combination of the right attitude and the right prayer? Was it God reinforcing the behavior He wanted to see from Bill? Did Bill, as Mitzi's husband, have a special authority given by

God to pray for her, and God was waiting for the right prayer and attitude from Bill? One thing is for sure. After the short prayer for Mitzi to see the truth of her situation, the truth was revealed only minutes later.

Epilogue

I cannot tell you that Bill and Mitzi's life together was smooth sailing, though they did have their good moments. A few of those moments included remarriage and children.

Wisdom tells me that many things in life are up to us. One of those things are relationships. It is most likely an overreaching prayer to ask God to make a relationship great. Instead, a better prayer may be to ask the Lord to give us wisdom about what makes a relationship good. What things about myself do I need to alter? Of course, we can't expect offensive or irresponsible behavior to be rewarded in a relationship, regardless of the amount of prayers requested. It is still up to us to learn how to pull together and put God's wisdom into practice.

What did I become convinced of? The Father's attentiveness to our heartbreak and willingness to help.

Discussion, Reflection, and Actionable Suggestions:

1. Are you at the end of your rope?
2. Do you have situations you need to give over to the Lord?
3. Do you have family members who God has given you responsibility to care for and you are at the end of your rope with them? Can you give them over to the Lord in prayer?
4. Do you need to ask the Lord for wisdom on what to do and say?
5. Do you need to take more responsibility for your own actions or inaction?

6. Is there a problem in your life that is not responding to prayer? Would you be interested in taking a spiritual inventory?[127] What needs to change?

---

[127] http://powerofhumility.org/?p=3150

21

Father, Tell Me How Much You Love Me

For God so loved the world.
-- John 3:16

"**F**ATHER, BESIDES JESUS DYING for me and you giving Him as a sacrifice for me, how much do you love me?"

Love Over Time = Sense of Worth

Jesus loves me, this I know, for the Bible tells me so. I guess the Bible telling me so should be enough to convince me of God's love, but one day I asked for more. I wanted more assurance from God Himself.

The Bible tells us that God, through Jesus' willing sacrifice, revealed the depth of His love.[128] And simultaneously, He demonstrated how much He hates the rebellion that lies within our nature, the rebellion that breaks relationship with Him.[129] So, with this one act of sacrifice, He deals with this rebellious (sinful) nature, as only God could, to ensure our survival and continued relationship with Him

---

[128] John 3:16
[129] I Peter 1:18-19

in Christ. It is a somewhat complicated, yet ingenious solution that could only be conceived in the mind of God.

I Need to Feel It

I have spent a lot of thoughtful moments trying to grasp this concept...to intellectually attempt to grasp God's love. On some days that is enough for me, but on other days it is not. Thoughts of His love for me usually stimulate my mind, but not always on a felt emotional level. I need to feel love from God. I want to know love and feel love.

Many argue our need to feel love gets us into trouble. The argument goes that love is a verb, an action word, something you do. But there is no denying that most of us desire, on a very deep level, to feel love. We desire to feel it because we have felt it. We know of its existence and how relationships have caused us to feel it. Like an addict wanting to feel the sensation again, so we too long to feel the sensations of love.

There is an old saying that goes, "To know you is to love you." We would all like to think that about ourselves. In so many words, Jesus tells us it is true. If He knows us, He will love us. Jesus creates a scene recorded in Matthew where He sits in judgment regarding a person's fitness for an eternal reward. Jesus reveals to a group who claim to know him: I never knew you.[130] What a sobering scene. Obviously, it shows that Jesus requires more than claiming to know Him, more than knowing about Him, and more than attending religious services in His name.

What Does Knowing Him Mean?

What does knowing Him mean? A love relationship thrives on two-way communication. Reading about a character in a book is

---

[130] Matthew 7:23

different from having a relationship with the character. One is static and the other dynamic. Reading about someone is static, while engaging in a two-way communication with someone is dynamic. I recently met a gentleman from Memphis who claimed to be Elvis' biggest fan. He is writing a new book about him. He also confessed he never met Elvis. So, he knew Elvis, but Elvis didn't know him.

The real question becomes, "Does the Lord know me?" Does the Lord love me, Clay Mize? This question enters my mind from time to time. Originally, I accepted this relationship because someone told me He loved me. Now, I journey on looking for additional evidence of His love. Is the evidence there for me? Is my love relationship growing because of the evidence I see that He loves me?

Let me back up a second here. It is not my belief God shields and insulates me from disappointment or any other maladies of a fallen world. As I have said before, I don't believe in a genie-in-a-bottle, wish-grantor God. That kind of relationship would go south pretty fast. I would become a selfish user, and He would become my slave.

I believe more in terms of a good, loving, and wise Father, with a son He loves. That kind of father is not just a wish grantor, because He understands our true need and how to develop character. This kind of relationship, over time, if understood, leads me to believe the Lord loves me.

What Kind of Relationship Do I Have with the Lord?

So what kind of relationship have I had with the Lord? It has grown as relationships do. It has developed and matured by our conversations and experiences together. I never feel alone. Our conversation is ongoing. He goes with me wherever I go -- including when I knowingly go where I shouldn't go, both mentally and physically.

Our conversations are certainly unconventional. He is not conversational like most people I know. I ask him questions and he gets back to me in time. He forces me to be patient and listen. I perceive He tests if I am really wanting to listen or not. I don't really appreciate this aspect of our relationship, but it is the way He is, or at least that is my perception of the way He operates with me. With that said, I do believe there are others who hear from Him better than I do and that our hearing can improve.

Sometimes His answers are so long in coming I forget I asked a question or made a request. Did I mention I don't really like that? But when He does answer, it makes a big impact on me. He has a way of getting His point across to me.

Our relationship reminds me of an adult with a child. We laugh at the impatience of a child. I can be like a child around Christmas with God. I feel like His answers never get here. Maybe we become a little more like God as we get older. What feels like a fleeting moment now felt like eternity as a child. I remember the presents being under the tree a couple of weeks before Christmas. The days could not pass fast enough, and my parents mused at my impatience. From God's perspective, a decade is like a moment. I am sure we amuse Him as we rattle the box, anxious of and for what will come.

Tell Me How Much You Love Me

The following story is one where the Lord did not wait as long to respond.

One day I asked the Father how much He loved me. Almost immediately a thought came to me, "I gave my Son for you." Good answer, I thought. The perfect answer. Sounded like God to me, so I chalked it up to God and that satisfied me for a while.

A few days later I asked again. "Tell me how much you love me." Again, the thought about Jesus' ultimate sacrifice came and how it proved the Lord's love for me. Then He added that it was not only Jesus who made a sacrifice. The greater sacrifice was a Father giving His Son for sacrifice. Proof of love from both Son and Father. That is awesome, I thought, and it satisfied me awhile longer.

More days passed, and I asked Him again, "Father, besides Jesus dying for me and you giving Him as a sacrifice for me, how much do you love me?" I realize this sounds like the question of a small child to his father, and I meant for it to. Immediately, I saw a vision of Him laughing at me, so I thought the question must be okay. So, I laughed, too, at the absurdity of the question.

Within a week, a female friend came to me and said, "I don't know why I am going to say this to you, but I believe God really, really loves you."

Immediately, I asked, "Why are you saying this?" She said, "I don't know, but I felt I needed to tell you."

"Whoa," I thought to myself, remembering my recent ask. "Could it be?"

A few more days later it happened again. An acquaintance got a strange look in his eye as he said, "You are very special to God."

Again, I asked, "Why do you say that?" His reply was, "I don't know, that just came to me."

"Wow," I thought, "twice in a relatively short time."

Within a couple more days, another friend said essentially the same thing as the first two. This third confirmation brought me to tears, for I knew it was no coincidence. The Father really did regard me special and loved me enough to respond to my childlike request.

The number 3 has a great significance. In Hebrew the number 3 is considered the number for permanence. If it happens three times, it is true and permanent. The three confirmations of His love for me will always be a treasure.

Underestimated

This exchange with my Father surprised me. Are you kidding me? I am a nobody except to a few family and friends, yet "The Father" reaches out to reassure me of His love simply because I asked him. What kind of Father is this? I understand why it is hard for some to believe, for it is so difficult to believe there is someone like Him.

His personal reassurance did for me what the Bible couldn't do. My new song is, Jesus loves me, this I know, for He told me so. I liked hearing it even better in person.

Of course, there is nothing that says I love you like opening His arms to fallen humanity on the cross. I hope you can see this, but why not ask the Lord how much He loves you? It might just improve your ability to listen and discern the voice of God.

Discussion, Reflection, and Actionable Suggestions:

1. Do you sometimes feel like the addict who needs to feel the sensations of love?
2. Do you need to have better communications with the Lord? If so, join me in this prayer: Lord, I want to have a better relationship with you. I want to know you better, and I want you to know me better. Help me to listen and to hear your voice. In Jesus' Name.
3. Have you stopped communicating with the Lord because He did not grant your wish? Do you need to ask him to forgive your wrong attitude? If so, join me in this prayer: Lord, I want to ask your forgiveness. I have shut you out because you did not

grant my request. Lord, I want to rekindle our relationship and grow close to you again. In Jesus' Name.

4. In this chapter, the author writes the following: "Tell me how much you love me." Again, the thought about Jesus' ultimate sacrifice came. How it proved the Lord's love for the author. Then He added it was not only Jesus who made a sacrifice; the greater sacrifice was a Father giving His Son for sacrifice. Proof of love from both Son and Father. Marinate a bit on this truth and discuss.

5. Are you willing, like the author, to ask the Lord to reveal to you in new ways how much He loves you? If so, join me in this prayer: Lord, like you did the author of this book, please reveal to me in new ways how much you love me. In Jesus' Name.

22

My Dad's Last Day

"All flesh shall know that I, The Lord, am your Savior, and your Redeemer, the Mighty One of Jacob."

-- Isaiah 49:26

I GOT A CALL FROM my sister Jeanette on my dad's last day. She called on a Wednesday night to say that Dad was in the hospital in Jasper experiencing heart pain. It came as no surprise due to his history.

The drive to Jasper took just under two hours, and on the way I envisioned giving his eulogy. I committed it to memory because I knew. He died that night, but not until after we looked into each other's eyes. There was a download that took place in that moment, and it seemed to satisfy us both. I could never ascribe a value to that transactional moment, for in his eyes I understood my own value as never before.

Eulogy for Gene Mize

The following came to me almost word for word as I traveled the winding country road between Florence and Jasper. I would deliver it at his funeral three days later. Looking back at the eulogy, the phrase "The Lord has been good to us" is like a refrain or a congregational response. These are the words that came to me:

First, I know Dad would appreciate the fact that his funeral didn't interfere with the Alabama–LSU kickoff at seven tonight. And I also know that he would be the first to crack a joke here today. To have Gene Mize with us for 84 years was a blessing.

The Lord has been good to all of us for letting us know him.

He married my sweet mother, and they were together forty years. They raised us and got us out of college before we lost her.

The Lord has been good to us.

A few years after losing her, two wonderful women came into our family -- Merita Howell and her daughter Sue Phillips. We quickly grew to love Nana during their years together, but then suddenly, it was her time to leave us too.

The Lord has been good to us.

After a few more years, another sweet lady comes into our family. At first, we worried it might not happen. A few months after Anna Stockton lost her husband, dad decided he would call Anna and invite her to lunch. She said, "Thank you for the invitation, but I had a husband and I am not interested in another one."

A couple of weeks later, my brother Elwyn came to visit. He said, "I am worried about Dad. He is depressed because Anna turned down his lunch invitation." Elwyn knew I kept a prayer journal, and God answers my prayers, so he asked me to pray that Anna would change her mind. I prayed and wrote it down in my journal.

Two weeks after the prayer for Dad and Anna, she called to say she had changed her mind about going to lunch. After that, a day didn't pass without the two of them talking or being together. A few weeks after their first dinner date, Dad said to me, "I was just hoping for someone to talk to, but this woman loves me. I told her about my failing health, and she said, "If we get nine days or nine years, I want us to spend them together."

June of next year, they would be married nine years. But if you count their courtship, they had nine years together.

The Lord has been good to us.

A couple of years later, in the same prayer journal, I prayed the Lord would allow Dad to keep teaching his Bible class until the day he died. He laughed at me when I told him about the prayer, but I knew he appreciated the prayer and the sentiment.

Only three weeks ago, my brother Joel made a special visit from Colorado and spent four quality days with Dad and Anna. They scoured the countryside, talking about family and the old days.

The Lord has been good to us.

Two and a half weeks ago, Dad and I went to visit the family around our old home place. We visited the Harp Place farm (they retained the name of its previous owner) he bought with his Dad Albert after coming home from WWII. When he moved to Double Springs, Alabama, after marrying Anna, he sold the place to his brother Wilburn. After a visit with Wilburn, he expressed how proud he felt with the improvements Wilburn made to the place.

That same morning, we spent several hours with his sister Footsie (Virginia) and brother-in-law J.D., before heading back to Double Springs. I started toward Hwy 278 back to Double Springs, and dad said, "No, I want to go through Haleyville. Haleyville is my town, and it always will be, and I like to see it."

The Lord has been good to us.

The next day he calls me to say he has won four tickets to the Alabama vs. Mississippi State game at his Lions Club luncheon. He asked if I would take he and Anna to the game. I was pleasantly surprised since he had shown no interest in attending a game in years. It was not a good game, but just like he liked them -- Bama won big!

The Lord has been good to us.

The following Wednesday, on November 12th, dad had his 84th birthday. Jeanette and Jim came home early from Ireland to celebrate his birthday. He got many birthday well wishes from kids, grandkids, family, and friends. I called to sing him *Happy Birthday*, and he bragged about finishing two homemade fried peach pies Anna had made.

The Lord has been good to us.

I asked him what he was doing on his birthday. He said, "I am teaching the Wednesday night bible class at Thornhill on Isaiah 46-49." This was his first time to teach the class since aneurysm surgery the previous November.

Teaching his class was his last official act on this earth. Do you remember my prayer?

The Lord has been good to us.

During his last few hours, in addition to Anna and I, my brother Gary and Linda were the last to be by his side.

The Lord has been good to us.

When sharing these God-incidences with my friend Mark Bates, he commented, "Sounds to me like he was taking a victory lap."

I think he was too. Thank you.

Epilogue

I prayed he would teach his class until the day he died because I had seen the heartbreak of Alzheimer's. I couldn't bear the thought of my father succumbing to this disease. So, I covered my fear and dread with prayer.

So, I prayed and journaled, "God, please allow my father to keep a sound mind until the day of his death. And even more specifically, Lord, please allow him to teach his Bible class until the end. He taught a class at church for at least thirty years, and I knew he loved that.

Time marched on, and at age 82, a doctor diagnosed an aneurysm in each leg. They explained he needed surgery immediately. The surgery was treacherous and recovery for a man of his age would be tough.

He survived the operation, but surviving the recovery became doubtful. Then a strange and upsetting thing happened. My dad lost his mind. He didn't know us and asked for things that didn't exist. He would grasp in the air for invisible objects of his imagination. It was a world of his own. His actions reminded me of others I knew suffering with dementia.

I was heartbroken and thinking about my prayer. It was discouraging, but then a really good thing happened. Suddenly, after four days, my father came to himself. I was astonished. The doctors explained that when a person experiences a lot of pain, they can display symptoms of dementia. It would have been nice to know that in the midst of our despair.

It is about a year later when I make the drive to the cardiac ER in Jasper. Dad's wife Anna, Gary my brother, and his wife Linda allowed me to take their spot in the ICU. Dad had the covers up to his neck and his eyes closed. I couldn't tell if he was sleeping or sedated. I went to the foot of the bed and put my hands on his feet. That is when our eyes met for the magical moment. His eyes said so much, but for sure, they said, "I think this is it...I am glad you are here...goodbye...1 love you...take care...make me proud...It's ok...I will live on in you." And when he finished, he closed his eyes again.

Within five minutes, the "big one" hit him. He writhed, stretched, and stiffened as if his body were hit by a jolt of electricity. He grunted like a man trying to lift a heavy weight. They asked us to leave the room, and I knew he wasn't going to survive this.

Within a few minutes, the doctor asked to see a family member, and I volunteered. He said my father was still alive, but that his heart had essentially exploded. "The machines are keeping him alive," he said. "It is up to the family how long we keep him on the machines." I asked if he had any chance of recovery. He said there was none. "Turn 'em off," I said.

I would never had imagined making that decision regarding the life of my father. It was sobering to tell Anna, Gary, and Linda that he was gone.

Then I thought of God. How he honored me and my prayer. How he had allowed dad to keep his mental acuity through 84 years. And how on his 84th birthday and the day of his death, he taught his last Bible lesson.

My brother Gary was in my dad's last class. It has been ten years since my father's death. I asked Gary if he remembered the lesson from that night. He said he determined to always remember that last lesson. He said it came from the book of Isaiah, Chapters 46-49. Fittingly, the last verse he ever quoted was Isaiah 49:26. It reads: All flesh shall know that I, the Lord, am your Savior, and your Redeemer, the Mighty One of Jacob.

Only God could write an ending like that.

Discussion, Reflection, and Actionable Suggestions:

1. Have you ever kept a prayer journal? Would you consider starting one?
2. Are there requests you would like to make of the Lord for family members or friends?

3. Do you have requests you would like to make of the Lord for yourself?
4. Have you ever had a time when the right words seemed to flow to you effortlessly?
5. Have you ever had a time when things seemed to work out as if the Lord were orchestrating it?

23

Tell Cher I Love Her

For God so loved the World that He gave His Only Begotten Son, that whosoever believeth in Him shall not perish, but have everlasting life.

-- John 3:16

"LORD, I NEED YOU to talk to me more than I need to talk to you."

One day it occurred to me I do all the talking in my relationship with the Lord. When I pray, I talk. Then it occurred to me, what do I have to say to the Lord that He doesn't already know? Shouldn't I talk less and listen more. That is what I decided to do. It was hard at first. Listening is hard. It takes concentration and attention. And it takes time.

There is an old smoky billiard hall not too far from where my office used to be. The Smokehouse is famous for their half-and-half stew (half chili and half vegetable stew) and greasy flat-grill cheeseburgers. Chuck, the long-time grill master, could turn out the food and Cher kept the orders moving.

This was not your high-class joint, but a place where two worlds met. It was the place where doctors, lawyers, and businessmen joined the commoner and the hustler for lunch and a game of snooker or pool. It was my favorite place for lunch and to people-watch.

Tell Cher I Love Her

One day my prayer was this: Lord, I need you to talk to me more than I need to talk to you. You are God, the Creator of the Universe. Let me listen and you speak to me.

Not long after the prayer, this is what I heard during my quiet time listening: Tomorrow, go tell Cher at the Smokehouse I love her.

When I asked the Lord to speak to me, I hoped He would give me some divine wisdom or revelation. I wanted something I could use to make me look wise and spiritual. But not this -- not to embarrass myself at my regular watering hole.

"Lord," I argued, "I don't really know Cher. Our only conversations involve ordering a hamburger or stew." My argument, I realized, was impotent, and I needed to muster the courage to tell Cher that God loves her.

Cher is a no-nonsense type of woman. She is a lanky six foot three inches tall, with big hands. It occurred to me she might have been good at basketball back in the day. When you give Cher your order, she yells it to Chuck. She makes things happen at the Smokehouse, but not much for small talk or schmoozing.

The next morning was spent working up my nerve. I envisioned myself going into the Smokehouse and seeing Cher across the counter, helping Chuck fill orders. Sitting on the bar stool, I would squeeze between patrons. *How awkward it is going to feel relaying this message to Cher surrounded by such a conflation of people who know us. There is no way around it. I might as well get it over with.*

So, during lunch, I trudged the two blocks over to the Smokehouse. It was crowded, and I was nervous. Like I envisioned, I squeezed into a bar stool at the counter. I looked for Cher, but I didn't see her. The waitress asked me for my order. "Hey," I whispered, motioning her closer, "Where is Cher?" "She is off today," she said.

Whew, what a relief. Grabbing a paper someone left, I looked for the sports section. About that time, the guy next to me got up to leave. Sitting on the other side of him was Cher. My eyes widened as our eyes met.

"I thought you were off today," I said. She looked at me strangely and said, "I am, but I came by for lunch." "Oh," I said, "God told me to come by today and tell you something." Now her eyes got big. It was just Cher and me. Everyone around us was preoccupied and no one was listening. "He told me to tell you He loves you." She looked back down at her food and said nothing. When she turned back to look at me, a big tear had formed in her eye. All she said was "thank you." I didn't really know what else to say, so I just shrugged. Silently, I ate my porridge, but I wondered what may have been going on behind the scenes in her life. Were my words the answer to what she had been asking for?

At the Altar

A few weeks later, while standing in the pew as my pastor gave his altar call, out of the corner of my eye I noticed movement down the aisle. It was Cher and she moved toward the altar. She looked up and our eyes met, as surprise registered on her face. We smiled at each other. What are the odds that she would decide to go to church and it would be my church?

A year or so later, I moved to another part of the city and to a different church. Cher was still there when I left. The Smokehouse changed management, and I didn't see Cher there after that. Though years have passed, I never forgot how my prayer confirmed my need to listen more than talk. It taught me that good things happen when we listen and obey.

Epilogue

My nephew Andrew is part of my team of advisors, helping me with edits and suggestions to make the writing better. It has been a few years since this incident with Cher, and he was curious about the incident and how the episode changed me.

Andrew: Did you and Cher have conversations or speak about this incident?

Clay: I wish I had gotten to know her, but I did not. We were cordial at church, but I never mentioned the incident to her, nor she to me.

Andrew: Did this experience make it easier for you to be patient and listen, or is it still as difficult as it once was?

Clay: I think it is easier now, simply because I believe God does want to communicate with us. At first, listening was like watching for a pot of water to boil. As long as you watch it, it never seems to boil. The moment you forget about it, it begins to boil.

Another way to say that is that I think my conscious mind gets in the way of my hearing from the Lord. Sports psychologists say for a player to get in the flow, he must get past his critical, conscious mind and allow the subconscious to take over and do what it knows to do.

I believe hearing from the Lord is like that. The conscious mind is too judgmental and can over-evaluate. It is quick to dismiss something it doesn't understand or doesn't fit its paradigm. I think our doubts about God come from there. Paul the apostle said that we are not to be conformed to this world, but to be transformed by the renewing of our mind.[131] I believe he was speaking of the conscious mind here. Too much network news, political correctness, and Hollywood scripts are all selling the vantage point of the world. We renew our mind with a steady diet of God's Word to fight off the world's view taking over our mind. It takes discipline and intention to do that.

I have not been as disciplined and intentional about my prayer life as I wish I had. There were several years that I kept a prayer journal almost daily. Somehow, I got out of the habit. My guess is I went through some major transition that rearranged my habits. I continued to journal some of my prayers, but not with consistency.

I have never stopped listening. Paul told the Christians at Thessalonica to pray without ceasing.[132] I think this means that we can always be in a state of praying and listening. Jesus said, "My sheep listen to my voice; I know them, and they follow me."[133] So yes, I hear things every day that sound like the Lord to me.

I recently began a prayer experiment to help me hear from the Lord more quickly. I have only been doing it for a few weeks, but I have committed to doing it for at least a year without being in judgment about it.

I have a big closet in my home. I have a standup desk where I can place my computer. First thing in the morning, I begin by going to a worship video on YouTube to prepare myself. There are lots of great worship videos by Bethel Music and Hillsong, etc.

After a time in worship, I simply ask God to speak to me through my thoughts. I go to the keyboard with my mind centered on the Lord. Most recently, I center my thoughts by seeing Him as the Lamb who

---

[131] Romans 12:2

[132] I Thessalonians 5:16

[133] John 10:27

was slain, standing before His throne. I see Him as disfigured, a sign of His great love for us.

I then begin to write whatever comes into my head without judgment. Thoughts seem to flow to me for a while and then they just stop. So far, it has not been more than a couple of paragraphs and usually doesn't last more than 5-10 minutes.

I have been impressed with this so far. Most of the writing has been very affirming -- the Lord telling me He loves me, not to worry, that He is working things out, etc., etc.

I Wish Things Were More Straightforward

Another of my advisor team, Jamey, who is in a small fellowship group with me, made the following statement:

Jamey: I often ask the question, why do things have to be the way they are? Why can't we just be informed straight up what we are supposed to do? But it is like we have to listen to the whisper of the wind in the trees and figure it out.

Clay: I do think most things are straightforward. I don't have to consult with the Lord about whether to steal, kill, or commit adultery. I don't need to consult Him to tell me if I need to pray, worship, give, and repay for wrongs I have done. However, life can be very nuanced. For instance, if the Lord wanted me to call Jim to check on him and give him a word of encouragement, then that is something where I must depend on a prompting from the Lord. To me, we need both straightforward instruction and nuanced instruction when it comes to some of the details where we need help.

Living this complicated life with only an obscure instruction manual, and without the help of the Mastermind, Designer, and Creator who understands our potential and purpose, would be onerous.

There is a design specification that we sometimes overlook. He designed us to need Him.

Discussion, Reflection, and Actionable Suggestions:

1. Doesn't it make more sense to listen than to talk to God?
2. The author was looking for some deep theological insight, but what he got was to tell someone God loved them. Doesn't that sound like God to you?
3. Are you willing to embarrass yourself in order to be a vessel of God's love?
4. Are you willing to listen? If so, consider this prayer: Father, teach me to be patient and listen. In Jesus' Name.

24

A Billion Dollar View

"DEAR LORD, I would like to have a little more room and a better view from my backyard."

My Wonderful but Cramped House

For over 20 years I lived at 920 North Wood Avenue, in the first house purchased in my new hometown of Florence, Alabama. It was a great little gingerbread house built in the 1920's. The craftsmanship was excellent, with built-in cabinets and beautiful hardwood floors.

It was one of two built by Jewish spinster sisters desiring homes next door to each other. The sisters saved a little on construction costs by sharing a driveway between the houses. The decrease in privacy this caused was of no concern to the close-knit sisters.

The house is situated on the most beautiful oak-lined avenue in our city. Wood Avenue is in the historical district as the first residential avenue. A few blocks down the shaded sidewalk and you are in the downtown shopping and dining district.

For a couple of reasons, I sold the lovely little place. The shared drive is not as practical if your sister doesn't live next door. There is very little space for guest parking. The neighboring houses are very close, with the lot only being fifty feet wide. On the other side was a neighbor with only ten yards separating us. The backyard was practically non-existent and what little existed ended in an alley.

There was space to build a small arbor in the backyard that I covered with a wonderful muscadine vine. I floored this small ten-by-ten space with brick pavers. It was a cozy little place for three or four friends to visit outside for conversation and grill a burger.

Prayer for Space and a View

A country boy at heart, I grew up near our farm. It is easy to miss the wide-open spaces, and I began longing for more elbow room and a little better view. The day came when I expressed that desire to the Lord. I simply said, "Lord, I would like to have a little more room and a better view from my backyard."

A Shift in the Trajectory of My Life

Promptly, I forgot about my prayer and went on about my business. A year or so later, my business began to wind down, and I needed to sell the office building. The market was soft for a 7,000-square foot, 120-year-old office building downtown. There were already several buildings vacant in the area.

Fortunately for me, the real estate bubble in California was bursting and a number of Californians were taking money out of California and reinvesting in the Heartland. They were seeking a more stable real estate market. One of those real estate investors offered me 25% more than I was expecting. It was good timing for me.

Now there was a new problem. Because of the real estate tax laws, I needed to reinvest the profits into additional real estate or pay a large tax. So, the search began for a real estate investment.

One advisor suggested I look for lake property since the beautiful Tennessee River runs through our city. Lake property generally holds its value, and it sounded like a good idea. My preliminary poking around was to get a feel and understanding for what a good value looks like.

After looking at a couple of properties, a river-dwelling friend suggested a house. It had been on the market for a while next door to him. The house was familiar to me from visiting my friend, and I thought of it as an eyesore.

A View with a House

The house is a 1950's ranch-style. It had a squatty roofline and ugly porous red brick. To make things worse, a power pole stood in the middle of the yard with an array of ugly black lines drooping to the house.

"Can't hurt to look," I said. "At least I will have another idea of lake property value." So, I set up an appointment to see the house.

Upon arrival, I parked in the drive and made my way toward the side entrance to the house. The closer I came, the more I began to get a glimpse of the view from the backyard. I walked right past the door and into a breathtaking view in the back. The house sits atop a 200-foot bluff overlooking the Tennessee River, Wilson Dam, O'Neal Bridge, and a riverfront park. Upon seeing the view for the first time, one guest commented, "There are billionaires who do not wake up to a view like this one."

I decided the view was worth the improvements I would need to make. Plus, the house was big enough to make one floor into a bed and breakfast and live on the other floor. I liked the idea of my house paying for itself.

Over the next few weeks, we worked out the details and closed on the house. I hit the ground running, making repairs and improvements. It was a considerable investment of time and money, but the location is good enough to hold the value of the added investments. Before long, I was loving the house almost as much as the view.

Then one day while taking in this magnificent view, I remembered my prayer. And I remembered how cramped I felt in the 50-foot lot, with no backyard and a view of an alley. "Lord, I would like to have a little more room and a better view in the backyard." Wow, I thought! My Father really knows how to answer a prayer.

You Are Invited

Look us up on Facebook at Muscle Shoals Music House to see a few photos of our view. There is one other thing about the house I didn't know at the time. The previous owners had been the Muscle Shoals Sound recording studio in the 1970's. It was the guest house. Some of the house's more famous guests were Bob Dylan, Stephen Stills, Glenn Frey, Eric Clapton, and many others.

Change Is Always Hard

Getting to the house with the marvelous view was not an easy one for me. It was predicated on closing the business that took 20 years to build, and the sale of a historic office building and a home I lived in for over 20 years.

In many ways, my identity was wrapped up in these places and organizations. They held many fond memories of people I loved. I grieved over these changes.

In a similar way, the Lord reminds us it takes a sacrifice of the old before transformation into the new. Our second most iconic symbol in Christianity is that of the empty tomb. It is from the plunge of death that we emerge in new birth. Remember, a great life was lived before His crowning achievement on the cross ended in death, and before He emerged as our Savior and King.

Is it time to transition from what is already past to make room for the Lord to give you something new? The thing I am learning is, being a child of this great Father, He has plans for us on the other side of every death, and every ending. He is not surprised with the circumstance we find ourselves in. We can trust and look for what blessings the Father has in store for our new beginning.

Discussion, Reflection, and Actionable Suggestions:

1. There are times when we pray and forget about it. Have you ever realized the Lord had a prayer and you had forgotten about it?
2. Sometimes our route to getting a prayer answered can take us through difficult times and places. Are you willing to be patient and trust the Lord?
3. Our second most iconic symbol in Christianity is the empty tomb. Sometimes we forget, for the tomb wasn't always empty. Through death comes new life. Are you ready to sacrifice the old to make room for the Lord to give you something new?

25

God Must Really Like This Cat

"LORD, YOU KNOW I have cat allergies and this kitten is alone now and needs someone to care for her. If it's me, you have to heal me from allergies!"

The following story is one of three out-of-the-ordinary personal healing experiences. Sometimes the Lord healed and it wasn't extremely dramatic. However, it is always more dramatic to the person healed.

Cats Kill Me

Cat allergies can be debilitating. For me, within minutes of being around a cat, my nose and eyes are watering. Then sneezing and feeling tired and achy all over begins. It takes four days of allergy medicine to feel better. For me, being in the vicinity of a cat was a no-no.

Cleaning Up the Land

A few years ago, I bought a few acres of land. It was overgrown and a huge clean-up project. The outside work was therapy.

A big part of the clean-up was cutting brush and scraggly trees, putting them in piles and burning the piles. It was an after-hours and weekend job, so some of the piles sat in place for months until I got around to burning.

One day I decided to burn one of the piles. Walking around the perimeter of the pile, I sloshed kerosene before I set it afire. The kerosene helps the brush pile heat up quickly to ensure the bigger limbs and trunks catch fire. With the pile prepared, a match does the trick and the pile quickly is engulfed in flames.

Standing back, I watched the blaze. Nothing is quite as mesmerizing as a fire. I can stare at a flame for hours. I watched the bonfire but kept an eye out for rogue embers jumping or flying to start its own fire nearby.

Unexpected Survivor

Suddenly, I caught a glimpse of something that didn't fit the scene. There was movement in the fiery pile. It was an animal...a raccoon or possum, I guessed -- but no, it was a baby kitten. I feared I set its home on fire. I looked for other survivors but couldn't find others.

She couldn't have been more than a few weeks old. Picking her up, I held her with an extended arm. She was shaking. I felt compassion for her and walked her to my truck, not knowing what to do next or what to do with her. So, I prayed.

"Lord, you know I have allergies and this kitten is alone now and needs someone to take care of her. If it is me, you have to heal me of allergies." I put her in the truck and stayed with the fire until it was safe.

As we drove home, I wanted to have faith in my prayer for healing, but I braced for an allergy. I expected my eyes to swell and itch with the sensation of tiny cat hair stuck under my eyelids. At anytime, my nose would turn red while achiness enveloped me.

Never did I experience any allergic reaction. I kept her until a friend fell for her and wanted to give her a home. Strangely, I never experienced a cat allergy again. I even became a cat lover.

I suppose there could be other explanations to the unusual shift in my body's reaction to cat dander. I began to wonder if the Lord's animals are more important to Him than I previously thought. They are all, no doubt, magnificent creations.

Our Work and Purpose

There is a less remarkable healing story told in three of the four gospels -- a story the Bible gives only two short verses in each gospel. It is Jesus healing Peter's mother-in-law of a fever.

All of us have had a fever. We don't normally get upset about one, unless the temperature is very high and prolonged. We usually take a couple of aspirins, rest, and wait it out.

When we think about the recorded miracles, we concentrate on the blind receiving sight, the lame walking, and the deaf hearing. These are maladies from which one does not normally recover. So why waste the ink telling us that Jesus healed a friend's mother-in-law from an illness that she would recover from anyway in a few days?

Maybe the Lord is giving us some insight about prayers for healing here. Matthew,[134] Mark,[135] and Luke's[136] stories of this episode are slightly different. In Matthew's version, Jesus sees she is sick. He touches her hand and the fever left. Mark recalls the disciples telling Jesus about her condition and He took her by the hand, helping her up, and the fever left. Luke's story is, the disciples ask Jesus to help her. He rebukes the fever and it left her.

All three stories paint a little different picture. However, there is one thing in each of their accounts that is the same. Immediately upon

---

[134] Matthew 8:14-15
[135] Mark 1:29-31
[136] Luke 4:38-39

feeling better, Peter's mother-in-law began to wait on Jesus and the other disciples.

Peter's mother-in-law was needed. She had a job to do and a role to play that I imagine gave her great satisfaction. I visited the ruins of this woman's house in Capernaum on the Sea of Galilee. It was a house with many rooms. It had walls of field stones once gathered from around the sea. It was in her house where the Jesus movement began. Jesus and all the disciples knew her and cared for her. She loved them and served them.

When we carry the needs of our sick friends to the Lord, should we also remember to pray for His will to be done regarding their role and purpose? And can we, like the Lord, rebuke a fever for getting in the way of His work and purpose? Jesus always seemed to speak and act with authority and boldness. Should we follow His example or the example of His disciples who turned to Him for help?

Lord, help us to know what to do when a situation arises when others need help and healing. Increase our faith. We are grateful for this story of how Jesus responded to a sick friend. I also appreciate the insight into the Father's love. Philip, a friend and follower of Jesus, once asked Jesus to show them the Father. Jesus replied, "Anyone who has seen Me has seen the Father."[137]

Discussion, Reflection, and Actionable Suggestions:

1. Have you witnessed or received a divine healing?
2. The Lord's Prayer states "for Thine is the Power." What does that mean to you?
3. What do you make of God healing the author's cat allergy?
4. Why do you think God told us the story of Peter's mother-in-law in three of the four gospels?

---

[137] John 14:9

5. Which do you think we should do? Should we boldly speak with authority to a sickness or ask the Lord for help?

26

A Gift for Healing

To each person has been given the ability to manifest the Spirit for the common good. To one has been given a message of wisdom by the Spirit; to another the ability to speak with knowledge according to the same Spirit; to another faith by the same Spirit; to another gifts of healing by that one Spirit; to another miraculous results...
-- I Cor. 12:7-9

"WE BELIEVE THE LORD is telling us there is someone here dealing with a neck issue. If you are, we believe the Lord wants to heal you today."

Faith Healers Were a Joke to Me

Our tradition taught miracles were unnecessary in God's new economy. We believed they were originally needed to authenticate Jesus as God and establish His Church. Once Jesus accomplished His mission to provide a sacrifice for sin and the apostles firmly established the church, they were no longer needed.

The belief that miracles ceased included healing. We believed in praying for the sick, but we mostly prayed for God's comfort or that God would give wisdom to the doctor. God's answers excluded the supernatural.

As a boy I scoffed at Oral Roberts when he urged the television audience to put their hands on the television. He said that God would use their act of faith to heal them. In jest, I would put my hands on the TV and say, "Heal me, Lord," looking for a laugh.

In high school I helped write a skit and played the character of Ernest Angley, a televangelist faith healer. Ernest was a heavy-set man who prayed for sick people on his Sunday television show. Before he healed them, he would cast out the demons causing their infirmity. If healing a deaf person, he would command, "Come out, you deaf spirit," as he whacked them on the forehead with his palm, knocking them to the floor (that is what it looked like he was doing to me). The afflicted person would claim healing while his family or friends jumped for joy.

In my opinion, it was a staged performance. These were not people with real conditions, but actors playing a role to deceive. Playing the role of Ernest Angley in the skit, I wore an oversized suit stuffed with pillows. During one scene, I go into the bathroom and shout, "Come out," as the audience hears a toilet flushing. Next, I burst out of the bathroom, having removed the pillows from under my suit. This illustrated what I thought of Ernest Angley. He was full of you know what.

My Neck Problem

By high school, I was giving my neck a chiropractic adjustment several times per day. It was always stiff from playing football. We had hundreds of helmet-to-helmet hits, butting like rams fighting for territory. I thought I was *Ram Tough*.

After high school, the tackling stopped, but not the need for an adjustment. The condition worsened, and sporadically, I experienced muscle spasms that gripped my neck and upper back. It happened mostly during sleep. After waking, I was marooned on my mattress unable to lift the weight of my head. It was sometimes hours before the muscles relaxed.

One day a new chiropractor entered the examination room with x-rays in his hand. He said, "Did you know you had broken your neck?" "No sir," I said, "what do you mean?" He hung the x-ray on a lighted board and said, "See the line on this vertebra? That is a hairline fracture. At some point you took a nasty blow." "I guess it happened playing football." He just shook his head and muttered, "Football."

Open to the Possibilities of Miracles

As mentioned in an earlier chapter, I had experiences that opened me to the possibility my theology was flawed. The healing of my minister's wife Janice was a turning point.

In my twenties, had you asked if I was healthy, I would reply, "Healthy as a horse." My neck issue was simply an aggravation.

Husband and Wife with a Gift for Healing

My new church, who believed in spiritual gifts, sponsored a retreat in Birmingham. For one session, the organizers invited a man and wife team recognized for gifts of healing.

My purpose for attending was to observe. There was no thought of personal healing. It didn't occur to me I needed healing.

The couple opened the session by telling us about their ministry. They related how the Lord had healed people they laid hands on and prayed for. After the introduction, they invited the Lord to be among us and heal those who needed healing.

A few people walked to the front of the chapel to ask for their prayers. These were people with obvious ailments we knew about. We joined in to pray for them.

After a period of prayer, the husband said, "I have an impression there is someone here who is suffering with a…" and then he would name a specific ailment. I knew a few who responded. Sometimes I knew the person suffered with the condition and sometimes I did not.

"We believe the Lord is telling us there is someone here with a neck issue. If you are, we believe the Lord wants to heal you today." I thought, what have I got to lose? Though I felt I was managing the discomfort, it would be nice to live without constantly adjusting my neck. I went to them for prayer.

They laid hands on me and prayed. I felt nothing miraculous. There was nothing special about their prayer, except their tone convinced me they had faith the Lord wanted to heal my neck.

Nothing Seemed Miraculous to Me

To be honest, I did not go away rejoicing like they often did when Jesus healed the sick. Instead, I went back to my seat and sat down. Afterward, I went about my business for the rest of the day…then the rest of the week…then the rest of the month. It didn't dawn on me that anything had changed.

Then one day it occurred to me I had stopped giving myself chiropractic adjustments. There was no longer a need to. And it was a year later when it dawned on me I had not suffered a muscle spasm since the prayer. It has been 25 years since the last back spasm and I no longer need to adjust my neck.

All I can tell you is this happened to me. It is not that I understand it, but I know I had chronic neck issues and after the prayer my neck problems disappeared. This episode…this answered prayer, changed my perspective and shaped me to believe that God still gives gifts of healing for the common good.

Epilogue

John is a dear friend and on my advisor team. John is the son of Greek Orthodox immigrants and became a Christian while he was in college at Ohio State. He has been a Methodist minister for almost 25 years and has a great love for the Lord and the lost. He shared the following with me after reading this chapter.

John: I am really concerned about how you left this chapter without telling how you now feel about Oral Roberts and Ernest Angley. I met both men, and they both had a profound impact on me as a college kid and a young Christian.

Clay: Tell me about your experiences.

John: Oral Roberts came to speak to my church in Columbus. Because of my relationship with our music minister, Randy Cutlip[138], I got to go behind the scenes and be around Oral Roberts. He was such a dignified man and gentleman. After meeting him, I listened to him whenever I could, and I feel he was very instrumental in my transformation as a Christian.

As far as Ernest Angley is concerned, I must admit I am weirded out a bit at his mannerisms and style, but I can't deny the impact he had on me. A year or so after college, I visited his church to see what it was all about. The service started at about 7:00, and he gave his sermon. After the sermon, he prayed for the sick. Many sick people visited his services.

During this part of the service, he points at me and says, "Young man, God wants to heal your eye." Just so happens I had something in my eye for a couple of weeks. I had tried to flush it out but couldn't get it out. After he spoke to me, whatever was in my eye was gone. A few moments later he walked down the aisle where I was standing, and I

---

[138] Randy Cutlip was a member of the music group *Three Dog Night*

began to stumble like a drunk man. People told me it was the presence of the Holy Spirit that Mr. Angley was anointed with.

After the service I wanted to meet him. He went into his office and this huge line stretched down the hallway to meet with him. I was the last one in line. By the time I got in to see him, it was 10:45.

He was so gracious to me. He asked how he could pray for me. I told him I wanted God's will for my life and wanted to bring others to Christ.

He said, "Okay, son, if that is what you want to do, then I want you to take these books to read. They will help you. To win others for Christ, you need to learn to be a holy person. And you must keep yourself sexually pure. You must live a holy life. Then he prayed for me.

I left that night being so impressed that he would spend that much time with all these people and then give me such an important word that has always stayed in the back of my mind guiding me.

So, when I read that these men were a joke to you, that upset me, because these were dynamic men in the Kingdom of God. I wanted you to say how you felt about them now.

Clay: By the time I had the experience with my neck, the ministry of both men were in decline. I never really listened to either men. However, I am now very slow to criticize anyone who ministers in the name of Christ. I remember how much I have learned and how much more I know I can learn. That is not to say that we shouldn't test what others teach. I believe we should always test everything. But when we don't fully understand the issues, we are better off to say nothing than to speak against a man that may be God's man.

No doubt these men demonstrated they believed in the love and goodness of the Father. Is there healing power in the Father's love? If we believe there is healing power in love, then yes.

It was our earliest parents who were deceived into doubting God's goodness. That doubt remains in the recesses of our minds and keeps us from drawing close. We all struggle to accept the Father has a humble and gentle heart that responds to those who cry out to Him.[139]

Instead of fear, if we could accept the Father as humble and gentle in heart, we would not fear approaching Him or trusting Him.[140] I believe the sooner we trust Him, the sooner His love begins the process of repairing the warp of the world and mending our broken hearts and lives.[141]

I am for anyone who leads us to His goodness, that works to restore us to normal, even as we resist like children refusing our medicine.

Discussion, Reflection, and Actionable Suggestion:

1. Do you have areas of your theology that needs updating?
2. Are there areas in your theology that you have a better understanding of God today than you once did?
3. Are there things you have said about another person's theology that you wish you could take back? If so, consider praying this prayer: Father, I have said things in my immaturity that I wish I had not said. If I need to make a direct apology to someone for something I said, please bring it to my memory and give me the courage to make it right. In Jesus' Name.
4. Do you have any special friends who really believe in prayer that you could ask to pray for you in time of great need? If not, consider praying this prayer: Father, I need people who I can go to for prayer. Help me to identify these people who are in my life and send others that I do not know. In Jesus' Name

---

[139] Israelites in Egyptian bondage
[140] Matthew 11:29
[141] Psalms 147:3

5. Do you need healing? Consider this prayer: Father, I need your healing touch. I want to be restored to health. Please heal me and send others who have a gift for healing to me that they, too, may pray for me. In Jesus' Name.

27

Laying On Hands

There are a variety of results, but it is the same God who produces the results in everyone.

-- I Cor. 12:6

"PLEASE, LORD, heal my hips."

To Each is Given

Paul's first letter to the Corinthians offers all types of instruction. Like so much of his writing, it too has been rife with controversy. But none as much as chapter twelve, where he instructs about spiritual gifts.

In verse seven Paul says, "To each person is given the ability to manifest the Spirit for the common good." Allow me to paraphrase....every Christian is given a gift from the Holy Spirit(God). He or she is to use the gift for the common good.

One of the gifts God gives for the common good is healing. The receiver must be willing to share for the common good. Notice two qualifiers here. The first qualifier is the person must receive the gift from God. The second is the receiver must act as a willing instrument to share for the common good.

Laying On Hands

No one fully understands the power and significance of laying on hands. The origin and practice are ancient. Jacob, in Genesis, laid hands on the sons of Joseph to impart a blessing.[142] Moses laid his hands on Joshua and he became full of the spirit of wisdom.[143] In ancient times, there was a connection between laying on hands and offering a sacrifice. To lay hands on an animal or even a person was to offer their life as a sacrifice to God.[144][145]

Jesus laid his hands on the sick and so did the apostles.[146] The early church elders continued the practice. The Lord even used followers without title to lay hands and impart the Holy Spirit.[147]

My Old Hips

In an earlier story I wrote about breaking my leg. What I didn't mention was the complications and long-term consequences of that injury.

The first couple of surgeries were unsuccessful, and in the end took four surgeries to repair the breaks. In all, the cast was on for 99 days. That is a long time to keep an ankle joint totally immobile.

Injury rehabilitation is so much better than it was in the 1970's. The number of rehab sessions I received equaled exactly zero. Luckily for me, within three weeks I was back on the basketball court and in the weight room. The doctor informed me my ankle may never have a full range of motion. He said I would favor the ankle joint at the

---

[142] Genesis 48:14
[143] Deuteronomy 34:9
[144] Leviticus 4:15
[145] Numbers 8:5-11
[146] I Timothy 4:14
[147] Acts 9:10-19

detriment of other joints, and especially my opposite hip. I could expect some arthritis in that joint eventually.

That was life. I played basketball for two seasons, and one more of football and tennis. A limp was hardly detectable. For years, I measured my range of motion and my left ankle joint consistently had about twenty percent less range.

On my twenty-eighth birthday I wanted a sports car. I bought a sleek Nissan 280ZX with T-tops. It drove like a dream. Low to the ground, it required you to climb out when you arrived.

A friend saw me climb out and after a few steps said, "That car is for young people." "What's your point?" I responded. "When you get out of the car, you walk like an old man." So what if I ached and grunted until I warmed up. This is just as the doctor foretold twelve years earlier. It was my lot in life to live with hip pain.

God's Prompting

Then one day I was driving to a business appointment in Huntsville when I had a spiritual prompting. This must sound strange, but I felt like God wanted to heal my hips. My memory is a little fuzzy about how I knew this, but I will never forget pulling the 280ZX over to pray.

Not only did I pray but felt compelled to put my hands on my hips as I prayed. I said, "Lord, I believe you want to heal my hips. Please heal my hips, in the Name of Jesus." Immediately, I felt what I can only describe as a warm sensation pulsing through my hips. It lasted for a couple of minutes, and that was it. The heat I felt was nothing more than if I had put Icy Hot or Bengay on them. All I know is that from that point I have not had hip pain.

Epilogue

That episode happened over twenty-five years ago. Not only have my hip joints not deteriorated, but at age fifty-five I became a certified professional tennis instructor. I stand on concrete for hours at a time. I am also a better player than I was at age twenty-five or thirty-five.

It has been many years since I did the flexibility test on my ankle joints. The last time the ankles still had about a twenty percent difference in range of motion. I did it yesterday as I was working on this chapter. At least with my naked eye, the flexibility of both ankles are the same.

Gift of Healing

Debbie is in my small fellowship group and heard me tell this story to our group. She asked the following;

Debbie: Do you believe you have the gift of healing?

Clay: There are no permanent health solutions in this world. Unfortunately, the world and most of Christianity attempt to stigmatize anyone who is recognized with a gift for healing. I have prayed for people who recovered and some who did not. Privately, I pray for all my friends who are sick. I pray for many of them in person too. I have been a part of laying hands on sick friends and anointing with oil. Many have recovered and some with serious illnesses.

I do advocate that church people call upon the elders of their church to lay hands on them and anoint with oil as is directed by Jesus' brother James in his book by the same name.[148] However, here is the tricky part. I am not sure I would call upon the elders if I knew they did not believe in God's willingness to heal in that manner. For a prayer to be effective, it must be a prayer of faith.

---

[148] James 5

Debbie: So, you believe there are things that hinder our prayers for healing?

Clay: Most definitely, and unbelief is a big one. But I believe there are many other causes too. Sin is the biggest cause. Before sin, there was no sickness or death. When it entered the world, it affects everyone, young and old, and even the innocent who have no sin. Sin is the contaminator, a blood disease passed down to all. Adding more and more sin into our system is like taking doses of poison that will kill you sooner. A person must deal with the cause (sin) in their life before they can hope to get better.

Debbie: Are you talking about a person becoming saved?

Clay: Yes. The antidote to our infection of sin is the blood of Jesus, which purifies us from sin.[149] But even after we are saved, sin committed by you and committed against you must be dealt with as a chronic problem. Christians continue to sin, get sick, and die.

The way the Christian deals with the chronic nature of his own sin is through confession. Apostle John tells us if we will confess our sins, the Lord will cleanse and purify us.[150] We deal with sin done to us through forgiveness. Dealing with sin is like dealing with a bacteria that is making you sicker.

Jesus warned a man that he healed that if he didn't deal with his sin problem that he might find himself sicker than he was when Jesus first healed him.[151]

Debbie: Are you saying some sins are worse than others?

Clay: As far as sins that are worse than others, sexual sin is the only sin that is a sin against our own body.[152] But common sense tells us

---

[149] I John 1:7
[150] I John 1:9
[151] John 5:4
[152] I Corinthians 6:18

that many sins lead to sickness. The obvious ones are drug and alcohol abuse, gluttony, habitual smoking, promiscuous sex leading to disease, etc.

Then there are sins that affect our mind and emotions. Unhealthy and sinful thinking, expectations, attitudes and passions of the heart can put our bodies under stress. That is not to mention the poor financial and relationship decisions these conditions motivate us to make, adding even more stress.

All this "life drama" often leads to negativity and worry. Combine all this and life is spiraling out of control. No wonder 1 in every 6 Americans is taking a psychiatric drug. Add another 25 million Americans who consume illegal drugs and the number goes to 1 out of every 4 Americans are medicating to bear their life. They are trying to escape the consequences of sin instead of dealing with them.

Debbie: It sounds like sin is still a big problem, even for the Christian.

Clay: No doubt. I think the Church has done a poor job discipling new Christians. We have not stressed the importance of separating ourselves from the world's mindset and values. Most new Christians are not taught to immerse themselves in God's Word and learn His way of doing things.

We continue to violate the things that keep us from thriving (living the abundant life). Jesus condensed the solution to thriving into two directives. Love God and love people. It may be condensed, but that affects our every move. Every sin, therefore, is ultimately a sin against love.

As humans, we only thrive (live an abundant life) when we are nourished and nurtured by many healthy and happy relationships. Until we properly value the relationships God has blessed us with, including our relationship with Him, then we will restlessly roam the earth looking for something to salve our sin-sick soul.

Debbie: What is the number one thing that would help people have better relationships?

Clay: My first book was how humility is the number one quality trait to better relationships. It is called *The Power of Humility-The Secret to Being Happy*, and if you really want to know the answer to that question, then that is a decent place to start.

Discussion, Reflection, and Actionable Suggestions:

1. Have you received the spiritual gift God has given you for the common good? If not, consider praying this prayer: Dear Father, I accept any spiritual gift you wish to give me for the common good. Help me to recognize it and give me the courage to use it for the common good.
2. Would you like for one of the spiritual elders in your life to pray for you and ask God to impart to you the gift or gifts He has for you? If so, consider praying this prayer: Father, I want to follow in the footsteps of Timothy and have spiritual elders pray for me regarding my spiritual gift. Would you lead me to these servants of yours to pray for me?

28

The Man You Intended

CHANDLER AND I were a match. Not a match in some serendipitous way but matched by Big Brothers Big Sisters. Big Brothers Big Sisters is a national mentoring organization. Chandler was nine when we were matched.

Big Brothers Big Sisters require the big brother to spend at least two hours per week with their little brother. Additional time together is at the discretion of the big brother.

After a few weeks we completed many of the conventional activities that usually come to mind. We went fishing, to a ballgame, to the arcade, pitched batting practice, and threw the football around the yard. It was fun but took planning and was not always practical.

Prayer for Chandler

Dropping him back home, I asked if I could pray for him. He said he would like that. Putting my hand on his head, I prayed a prayer like this: "Dear Lord, please bless Chandler. Help him to grow up to be the man that you want him to be. Teach him to be a man after your own heart.[153] Give him a good night's rest, bless him at school, and give him

---

[153] Acts 13:22

favor with his friends and teachers. In Jesus' Name, Amen." This became part of our routine.

Coffee Group

In time, we started to do more mundane things like going to Wal-Mart or the grocery store. Chandler seemed to like that as much as fishing. He was a fun little companion, and we began to do adult things like meet with a group of men for coffee. He loved the reaction he received from the waitress and the other men when he ordered coffee.

Chandler enjoyed being around men and the men liked him. The men were sensitive to his father need and responded by taking interest in him and giving him special encouragement.

The coffee group's mantra was, we talk about three things: God, football, and women. Since we didn't know much about women, we talked mostly of God and football! The coffee group, I later realized, was a mentoring group for men seeking spiritual answers to the complications of life. Much of my theology we pounded out over coffee.

Any person could ask a question or name our discussion topic. Often, someone came in with a verse from the Bible and ask, "What do you think this is talking about?" Everyone would weigh in with a thought or idea, and occasionally we would come to a consensus.

It didn't take long to discover Chandler loved these coffee discussions, and even at age nine, would put in his two cents worth. Sometimes he sounded like a little kid, but sometimes his grasp and insight were quite astonishing.

What is the Lord Teaching You?

Chandler loved to be asked about what the Lord was teaching him. I was always amazed how quickly he could answer. It was evidence of an internal dialogue going on underneath the surface. He could always answer in a meaningful way.

Even before inviting Chandler to his first coffee group discussion, at age nine I asked him this question. I was curious how he would respond never having heard it before. So, one day while floating on rafts together, I popped the question, "Chandler, what is the Lord teaching you in your life?" He wasn't caught off guard by the question. He was thoughtful for a moment and said, "I think He is teaching me I need to be more respectful of my mother."

I was astounded and thought to myself, "God is talking to this boy and he already knows how to listen." I thought again about the genius of the question, teaching children to develop an ear for God.

Our talks after that day spread to many subjects, from sports to girls. However, they eventually included, "What is the Lord teaching you?" Our many conversations were rich and thoughtful. They developed our relationship in a deep and meaningful way. Though there is almost thirty-five years difference in our age, we became friends.

It Takes a Village

Chandler is now twenty-five years old and a graduate from Faulkner University, with a degree in Bible and a minor in counseling.

Chandler was deprived of many things most advantaged kids he grew up around take for granted. He had no brothers and sisters. His father was not in his life or around to provide financial support. Money was scarce.

His mom was a good manager, even though she always struggled financially. An example of her skill was to secure scholarships for Chandler to attend twelve years in a private Christian school. Mars Hill Christian school contributed greatly to his spiritual formation and served as part of the village that raised Chandler.

Chandler thrived in his school, though populated with mostly middle and upper middle-class kids. During his senior year, Chandler's classmates elected him as their senior class president. Little does he know, but this position of honor goes with him the rest of his life, as his class look to him for leadership as they reassemble for reunions in years to come.

When most kids were going to summer camp or playing ball, Chandler was going to a camp for future ministers and acting as a camp counselor at Maywood Christian camp.

Once in college, Chandler continued to chart a unique course. He spent three months studying abroad in Italy, Turkey, and Israel. He has been on missions to Central America and Africa as he continues to grow as a minister. Even in college, he continued to have favor with teachers and classmates who voted him homecoming king his senior year.

Did God answer my prayers to bless Chandler. So far, it is a big YES!

Epilogue One

My friend Joey and I built a lasting friendship sharing conversations over cups of coffee and now emails. He is part of my advisory group. He asked me the following:

Joey: What did God teach you through your prayers for Chandler?

Clay: I think it was comforting for Chandler to hear me pray for him on those nights I dropped him off. Over time, I believe he began to trust the Lord was hearing my prayer and it gave him confidence to pray. Our conversations kept me informed on where he was spiritually.

I suppose what I have come to believe is that even though we pray for the Lord's will and for His help, it was still ultimately up to Chandler. He had to develop his own trust relationship with the Lord, and it could have gone either way. There may be some benefit in modeling that trust before a child.

Epilogue Two

Mark and Joe are on my advisor team. After reading this chapter, Mark said I was leaving out an important part of this story. Joe said, the most important story in the book was the one I was unwilling to tell.

I said in an earlier chapter I had an unanswered prayer that was still too raw to write about. It is about me missing out on a very important part of my life. When everyone my age was getting married and building families I couldn't seem to pull the trigger. And it appears to be all my fault and that is embarrassing.

I heard all the single clichés. I have heard "you are too picky" to "when you stop looking you will find her" to "when you surrender what you want, God will give you what He wants" blah blah blah. Those have run over and over in my head like a bad virus on your computer that won't shut down.

I have speculated as much as my friends and family, but I don't have a good explanation other than taking the counsel of my fears. Possibly I didn't have the faith that I could keep my end of a covenant promise of loving no matter what. Marriage in America doesn't have such a great track record and as a quasi-pastor to a small group, I have talked many broken-hearted people down off the ledge with negative emotions so strong I worried if they might kill themselves or someone else.

I know that our hearts get broken and disappointed and we react in unhealthy[154] ways to ourselves and others. And then there is the

---

[154] When God crossed Cain, he made God pay by murdering his brother.

possibility this is my trial to either bruise my proud heart or test the resolve of my faith in the Lord.[155]

Sometimes I want to pretend that all suffering is the result of a moral failing. We know that is not so, for the Lord was known as a man of suffering, even prior to his crucifixion, so suffering is sometimes just a part of life. Seems like everyone has something and this is my something.

I had great opportunities to have it all. Certainly, the good Lord gave me multiple chances and great choices. I couldn't have been happier with those He sent my way and many great memories. I still have love in my heart for many I had the honor of knowing. My sister likes to say that I could never find someone that lived up to the standard of my mother. She was wonderful, and I was young when I lost her. However, that explanation is still unlikely.

Then, maybe, my character defect is even worse than I suspect. Maybe my selfishness is worse and outside the normal range. Maybe I took selfish advice from Hollywood along the way and romanticized too much.

I think the thing I have missed about the story of the cross is that it is a relationship story. It is the ultimate illustration of what it could mean to be in a love relationship. That kind of love is willingness to give our life for another. It is the understanding that true love may kill you, but it doesn't fail. In a way, it is understandable that our self-protecting selves would hesitate to put ourselves into that kind of relationship. But, wouldn't marriage be a more noble institution if people willingly entered in with this idea in mind?

Though I have swam many a mile in the sea of regret, it is hard to feel sorry for me. The single life has not been totally miserable for me

---

[155] The trial of Abraham when God asked him to sacrifice his son of promise

and there are some benefits to freedom. There have been some good times and good people I have met through it. I have experienced a lot.

Though there are many benefits to a nuclear family, my most raw regret is not being a father. I took for granted I would be and that disappointment has felt like someone wrapped my heart in 36 grit sandpaper. It can be a sore subject.

I love being around kids, so I decided to look for a way to get involved in helping kids. I met John Croyle through a morning television show I hosted and decided to visit him at the Big Oak Ranch for children. I told John about my desire and he asked me if I wanted to fish or cut bait. I never understood that expression until that day. He was asking if I wanted to help others who were working with kids or if I wanted to be hands on. I said, "I want to fish." He said, "Then find a fishing hole."

Later that month I approached Big Brothers Big Sisters about being a volunteer. They matched me first with Chandler (age 9) and then two years later with Hunter (age 6). Their situations are quite different, but I have loved both boys immensely. Just last week, Hunter and I went to eat at his favorite Mexican place to discuss his future plans. He finished high school last spring and is struggling to find his place. He blessed our food, and he thanked the Lord for his best friend Clay. I can promise, that blessed me.

Just yesterday I received news that Chandler is getting married. He asked me to be his best man. I couldn't feel more honored.

In addition to these two, I have been blessed with a number of young friends who seem to enjoy our conversations. And as of late, there are even a few boys and girls that I have the pleasure of sharing my love for tennis as their coach.

The good Lord continues to bless and redeem the disappointments I have experienced. I still have raw moments, and I still ask for help. I ask that He heal the regret I feel for how I handled the opportunities

He gave me and for not being the man He intended.[156] I ask Him to heal those I hurt and discouraged. I ask Him to help me redeem what is left of my life. There is still a chapter to write.

I have wanted to get angry at someone besides myself, and the Father would have been an easy target, but the truth is, I can't deny the Father's kindness and help to get me through some of the pain and regret.

Discussion, Reflection, and Actionable Suggestions:

1. Do you pray for and with the children in your life? If not, will you make a decision now to change that by committing to pray with the children in your life?
2. Do you have people in your life that are helping you to grow the spiritual side of who you are? If not, consider praying this prayer: Lord, I need people that will help me to grow spiritually. Please lead me to these people who can mentor me spiritually.

---

[156] I believe regret can make you physically ill.

29

Prayers of the Ego

A FEW YEARS AGO, I found myself at yet another crossroad. My successful business was interrupted by both a shift in the marketplace and a shift in state and federal legislation. I was being forced to start over. Did I really want to do that, or did I want to reinvent my career? I wasn't sure, but I began searching for the next big thing for my life.

I tried a few things that seemed to closely fit my skill set and expertise. That seemed logical and sensible. Nothing took hold or excited me. I began to wonder if I should consider more radical change.

There were some big dreams that I had kept tucked away on the shelf for years, never finding the time to follow them. These were ambitious, life altering dreams. So, I decided it was time to put up or shut up. On News Years Day I sat down with a clean sheet of paper and decided to write out my top audacious dreams and pray over them.

Many of the success gurus stress the importance of writing down your goals and dreams. They claim there is some magic in the process of writing things down, so you can see them with your own eyes.

On New Year's Day I determined to discover if these dreams were real or just pipe dreams. I decided to begin every day for a month writing out these dreams fresh with a clean sheet of paper. It would be a top 10 list. I wanted to know if I felt as strongly in a month after adding this intensity.

In the meantime, I would work on setting shorter term goals and developing plans to make the goals and dreams come true.

In only a few days I discovered a few things on the list were not as important as they were on the first day. They looked good on paper, but by day nine or ten it was obvious they didn't belong so I narrowed the list.

I realized that some of the dreams were too grand to be worked on consecutively. They would require a huge commitment of time and energy. However, I continued to come in every day and rewrite the dreams and work on plans that would help me achieve them.

On the last day of the month, I decided to continue it for another 30 days. At the end of the second month I had an epiphany. I realized I despised the thought of giving my days working on the items on the list. I especially wasn't interested in what I had considered my top two or three. For years I had imagined myself in these roles and now the thought repulsed me.

What had happened to me? The realization hit me that the top two or three on the list represented my ego. They were what I now call ego dreams. They were dreams that made me look good to myself and others and not so much what I was created to do.

Heart Dreams

I then differentiated ego dreams and goals with what I began to call heart dreams and goals. I knew what my ego wanted. The ego wanted to be and look important. It wanted me to do something others would be impressed that a person like me could accomplish. Maybe I would even impress myself or reinforce what I believed about myself.

I had no idea what my hearts dreams were. I then decided to go another 30 days and instead of writing out my ego dreams and goals, I would ask my heart what it wanted and write those down. I wasn't sure if my heart knew how to answer, but to my surprise my heart knew exactly what it wanted.

The ego dreams I am embarrassed to share, because they were so grandiose. The heart goals are less material or measurable, but they feel more right and they help to direct my decisions. Before, I begin a new task, I ask if it lines up with my hearts goals. If it does, then I move ahead.

I am not ashamed to share my heart's dreams and goals. They are;
1. To enjoy my life.
2. Be valuable, trusted and respected by my inner circle.
3. My actions demonstrate a loving person lives in here.
4. To be a positive force for good and outmaneuver negativity.
5. To discover what I have to offer that others want and need.
6. That my life will be transformed by my relationship with the Lord.
7. To be full of faith and optimism for the future for myself and others.
8. Be joyful as I do my daily tasks.
9. Be fun to be around.
10. To be at peace with the God of the Bible and my concept of myself
11. To be a person who connects, communicates and contributes from who I am.
12. To stay focused on the truly important things.

What happened next....
- I put to bed the notion of reviving all or part of my Financial Services business.

- I laid aside the audacious ego dreams and goals that I discovered repulsed me.
- I did complete one of the ten from my original list. I wrote about how mastering five key relationships is a guarantee to becoming happier.
- I turned my home into a bed and breakfast and entertain guests regularly.
- After being a volunteer tennis coach, I decided I loved teaching the sport, so I went through the rigors of becoming a USPTA professional instructor. I have about 20 kids that I teach weekly.
- I have put more energy into my small fellowship group who I pray for and where I am one of our leaders.
- My relationship with the Lord is deepening.
- I have rekindled dormant, but very important relationships.
- My relationships with my inner circle are not perfect but are flourishing and that makes me happy.
- And of course, I have been busy writing the book you are now reading.

I have found that I am quite busy and still maintain a good margin for doing the things I enjoy with people that are important to me.

Though the book title insinuates I am a nobody, I never thought of myself as a nobody. I measure my value by the measure the Lord used. He exchanged His life for me. This measure of value would stand, whether He ever answered one prayer for me, and I would be eternally grateful. Yet, He has answered the prayers in this book and many others.

Take time to remember what He has He done for you…

About the Author

Clay Mize roots run deep in the southern soil. He can trace his ancestry back to the American colonist, and native Cherokees creating a family with no sense of being immigrants. They fought in the Revolution, on both sides of the Civil War, and in World Wars I and II.

The closest his family comes to fame is through baseball. Ty Cobb and Johnny Mize are distant cousins who both played for the New York Yankees and are both in the MLB Hall of Fame.

Clay's mother and grandfather taught him the importance of learning to love work. Growing up on the family farm, by age ten he already understood the meaning of a long row to hoe.

In the early years, in addition to the family farm and football, he worked as a furniture assembler, lifeguard, paper boy, waiter, cookie salesman, and oil field roustabout. In the middle years he was an owner and CEO of an insurance brokerage firm, University teacher, and talk show host. In his latest phase he manages real estate investments and a Bed and Breakfast, and is an author, speaker and coach.

If you wish to contact him, you can email him at Claiborne.mize @gmail.com or call him at 256-436-9990.

www.ingramcontent.com/pod-product-compliance
Lightning Source LLC
LaVergne TN
LVHW041612070426
835507LV00008B/201